LAST DAYS
& END TIMES

- MAKING THE CONNECTION -

WHAT JESUS SAYS ABOUT THE FUTURE...

Peter Sammons

Christian Publications
INTERNATIONAL

First published in Great Britain by
Christian Publications International
("CPI") an imprint of
Inspiration – Assurance Publications
PO Box 212 Saffron Walden CB10 2UU UK

www.christian publications-int.com

Readers are encouraged to compare assertions in all CPI
books with the clear witness of Scripture. CPI offers this book
as a contribution towards continuing study of the
inspired Word of God, which the publisher considers to be
the final 'court of appeal' in matters of faith and doctrine.

ISBN 978-1-913741-10-5

Printed in Great Britain by Imprint Digital, Exeter
and worldwide by Ingram-Spark

WITH THANKS

With profound gratitude to our Lord and Saviour, in Whose
eternal Name all this material has been
assembled as an act of worship and adoration.

With grateful thanks my wonderful wife, Joyce,
for all the inevitable sacrifices you have made as this book
was prepared, and to our wider family.
Also to other Christian brothers and sisters
whose prayerful interest and challenge has been so helpful.

With thanks also to certain Christian brothers who have met
via the ubiquitous 'Zoom' facility in the past two years exploring
the theme of Last Days and End Time. You know who you are!
No names, no pack drill, as the military used to say!
We pray the glory goes to the triune God, the Saviour of the World.

IN MEMORY OF

David Henfrey, Dec 1955 to Aug 2017.
A lovely Christian brother,
who's gracious legacy funded this
and other Christian books.

To God be the glory . . .

PREFACE

The central acclamation of the mystery of faith, *'Christ has died. Christ is risen. Christ will come again'*, unites Christians across traditions, times and cultures as we proclaim the Gospel, we worship, share bread and wine, and seek to be faithful disciples within the complexities of life. This acclamation reminds us that we are rooted in time - the past, present and the future. Firstly, that our faith is rooted in the past, namely in the redemptive actions of Jesus (Yeshua), especially His atoning death. Secondly, that our faith is rooted in the present, namely in the reality of the presence of the risen LORD and the outworking of the gifts of the Holy Spirit today. Thirdly, that our faith is rooted in the future, in what is yet to be, namely the Second Coming of Jesus and the full establishing of God's Kingdom promises.

It is this future dimension and direction of travel which is often lacking in Christian teaching and proclamation today. Therefore, this book is timely, important, and valuable, for it carefully and reflectively explores what the Bible teaches about the Second Coming of Jesus and the consummation of God's promises.

Peter Sammons writes with a clear reverence for and obedience to the Biblical texts, focusing on key texts such as Daniel, Ezekiel, Zechariah, and Revelation. Space is also given for a careful study of Jesus' teaching in Matthew 24. In dealing with these texts, the author aims to help prepare disciples of Jesus to live faithfully today, and to be ready for what lies ahead. The author does this without being overly dogmatic and approaches this with caution. He understands that there is no definite detailed 'road map', yet does not hold back from stating what he sees as the clear truths of the Bible, namely a pre-millennial structure. It is for the reader to carefully study and reflect, and decide to what extent they find such a structure compelling and convincing.

I am particularly thankful to the author for the emphasis placed on affirming Israel's central role in the outworking of God's purposes and promises. This is a foundational Biblical truth which is sadly often ignored or misplaced. Sammons also shares many other significant insights; firstly, in terms of making connections between the seven Biblical festivals and the ministry of Jesus and His promised return and rule. Secondly, providing a clear distinction between the 'Last Days' and the 'End Times'. Thirdly, providing a focus throughout on the Gospel and how the coming events of the 'End Time' will impact upon the Gospel, the Nations, the Jewish People and the 'Church'.

Sammons is surely astute in realising that exploring such big issues can easily lead into many side-issues and nuanced controversies. Such side-issues and controversies seem only to divide and confuse. I think the author does well in avoiding being drawn into these issues and being unhelpfully sidetracked. He does this by seeking to focus on clear signposts and key questions, and for this reason many will benefit from this thoughtful and challenging book. I am certainly one of the many! As one of the many, I have gained new insights, and I also have several new, emerging and pressing pastoral, political and theological questions; however, above all I have a renewed trust in God and His Gospel, the Gospel of the crucified and risen LORD, which brings grace and truth and enables us to cry out 'Amen, Come Lord Jesus'.

Rev Alex Jacob M.A, M.PHIL
CEO, The Church's Ministry Among Jewish People.

CONTENTS

GOD SIGNALS . . .

GOD STEPS IN . . .

FOREWORD

**gather around so I can tell you what will happen to you
in days to come (Genesis 49:1).**

Being Aware

Jesus told His disciples to be aware of the times in which they are living, and to be ready for *the end of the age*. Matthew chapter 24 is the key passage in this regard, but signposts pointing towards *the end of the age* are peppered throughout Scripture. This is indeed a persistent theme in the Bible. True disciples are to be ready. For those outside the Kingdom the end will come "as a thief in the night"; in other words, they will be unprepared and so unready. But it will be different for the true Disciple of Christ.

Each generation has wondered whether theirs was the final generation, and often with very good reason. Wars, disease and famine – often in combination – have frequently seemed to 'fit' the signs of which Jesus warned. Furthermore, the world's broad and often egregious rejection of its Creator God, accompanied by stiff-necked pride and appalling sin manifested in so many ways, and so very often coinciding with persecution, war, famine, pestilence and moral decay, has left believers in each generation asking "is this the time?", "is *this* the rebellious generation that will bring upon itself final judgment?" And "are we *now* seeing the signs?"

Peter Sammons' mother, who lived through the London Blitz, told him that she wondered whether Hitler was the Antichrist and the European war the beginning of the great tribulation. Earlier generations wondered precisely the same of Napoleon Bonaparte and the horrors he unleashed. Each generation has had its own evil genius who acted in an 'antichrist' manner. Of course the early post-apostolic church wondered precisely the same about Emperors Nero and Diocletian and it seems in New Testament Scriptures that there was a palpable sense that *the end* would transpire within the lifetimes of their writers.

We must note, embarrassingly, that each generation since the time of ***Jesus*** *the Messiah* has had its 'prophets' who boldly proclaimed a particular time, set of circumstances and sometimes even date upon which 'the end' would come, only to be serially disappointed – but seldom abashed! Unsurprisingly the world at large has looked with derision upon *prophecies of the end* and concluded that the semi-permanent cry of "wolf" amongst religious people means that it is all bunkum, and best avoided. They forget too easily that the devil has a powerful incentive in raising up *false* prophets to discredit the clear and unmistakable message that one day the end WILL come and we all need to be prepared . . .

In this book we argue that one reason for the serial misunderstanding of *the time of the end* has been the institutional church's[1] divorce (we think this is not too strong a word) from the Hebraic root of the Christian faith, which led to a repeated inability to accurately "read the signs" of the times. Without understanding of God's ongoing purposes for Israel (and indeed actively working against His ancient people) the "church" has too often misread the signs. Viewed through the lens of God's ongoing purposes for this ancient people group, the signs are easier to decipher.

Are we in this book about to unveil a date, a time, and the perfect answer to the legitimate question – *when will the end come*? The answer is assuredly 'no', we will not. But we do argue that Jesus gave us very clear instructions of which we are to be aware and upon which we are to focus our attention and ultimately to take action when the time is right.

A second outcome of the 'divorce' of the institutional church from its Hebraic root has been its inability to distinguish properly between *the last days* and *the end time*. In this book we seek to shine light on this subject and enable readers to get this clearer in their own minds.

Had our Lord Jesus stated plainly "I shall return in 1,000, or 2,000 or 2,200 years" then it seems likely that the Christian faith would have died as soon as He had uttered such words. Each succeeding generation would have considered, in effect, that the Lord's return was nowhere near and so "we can live life as we see fit" - or, "eat, drink and be merry, for the Lord is not coming any time soon!" Such a disclosure would have been immediately and profoundly self-defeating. Furthermore, Jesus did drop a very broad hint that His return will be long delayed (that is, long delayed by our reckoning, as God operates outside of the dimension of time as we understand it). We are thinking here of Matthew 24:48 – but read the passage from verse 42 to 51 to get the context.

---

1 The "church" in its various institutional forms does not always coincide with God's purposes and revelation.

The Bible

How does your author view the Bible? As a writer I use the Bible as my primary resource in understanding God's revealed purposes, so I need to make clear my precise understanding of the 66 books that God has graciously given to Mankind as *canon*. I believe quite simply that God has made His purposes known, with clarity, in the Word that He has given. That does not mean that His Word is always easy to understand and apply, but it does mean that the diligent seeker after truth will find what he or she needs in the pages of Scripture. Ultimately our ability to understand what is given through the Bible is dependent on our relationship (or lack of relationship) with the wonderful Holy Spirit who inspired its words and who enables and assists us to understand.

I have written elsewhere about the Bible itself, and *this* book is not the place to revisit such questions. If readers have difficulties with the Bible *as the revealed Word of God* then they may, and are encouraged to do so, pursue their own enquiries with the Bible itself, and with other able writers[2]. Right now the simple assertion is made that *you can depend on what God has provided, and the Bible tells us everything we need to know* – not necessarily all we might want to know! – concerning God, His relationship with humans and His ultimate purposes.

Who might read this book?

Most people have some interest in the future, if only for purely self-centred reasons. On that basis much of the subject matter of this book will have a degree of broad interest and relevance. The book is written, first and foremost for those **disciples** who love Jesus as Lord and as Saviour, who trust Him for their future and would like to better heed Jesus' warning to be ready for what lies ahead. Jesus said "***my sheep listen to my voice***" (John 10: 27). The sheep of any flock come to know the authentic voice of their shepherd. They will listen out for and follow that voice, which leads them to sustenance and to safety. They will be rightly suspicious of other voices. They will search diligently for what Jesus has said about the future.

Jesus warned about 'hired hands' – shepherds who were only working for a wage and who will abandon the sheep (John 10:12) when it seems convenient for them to do so. We would be foolish to assume that these are just throw-away

---

2 We would add, and with various online video material such as the valuable work of David Pawson and Mike Winger. In addition, the graphics of the bite-sized episodes provided by **The Bible Project**, are really helpful mechanisms to help bring alive the Bible to a generation less comfortable with dense text.

lines from our Lord; He spoke them for a reason. Christians are only to follow the authentic voice – we are only to follow the true voice. This is not to suggest that Christians will be monotone, template cut-outs, all looking the same, thinking the same and doing the same things. That is emphatically not what Jesus is looking for. But there comes a time when declared beliefs depart so markedly from revealed truth that they become a non-authentic expression of Christianity. Jesus told us to be prepared for our future. Your author trusts that, in some small way, *this* book may help Believers to be prepared for that future and properly to understand and interpret the times in which we live today.

Disciples (Believers) who want to understand the times in which we are living today *and will face tomorrow*, are those for whom this book has primarily been written, with the prayer that it will help them to make sense of what is true, what is false and to make their own dispositions accordingly.

Others may read this book: those who are avowedly 'liberal' in biblical 'interpretation' may pick it up, if only to find ways to counter it. If you are one of those **liberal** readers, then you are more than welcome. We would suggest, though, that the challenge for you personally is not to adhere to, or agree with, what your author may be saying, or what any other author may say, but rather to try with honesty and integrity to listen to the authentic voice of Jesus. He was known in the time of His earthly ministry as "Master" and is now known as Lord and as God (John 20: 28). As a liberal, are you *really* prepared to listen to Him? And where He pronounces with clarity and directness, are you prepared to obey?

Some on the fringes of Christian belief, such as Mormons and Jehovah's Witnesses[3], may also be intrigued by what is explored in this study, comparing it to what their own 'sacred writings' profess. Finally those who belong to 'the religions' might stumble across this book and sense that Jesus may be able to speak into their own situation. The future is as real and as relevant to those of **the religions** as to anyone else. If you are of non-Christian religious persuasion, then again you are especially welcome to consider what is being explored in this book, as it reveals the future of all human-kind, not 'just' the future of Christians.

It is most unlikely that **atheists** will read this book, unless again they are seeking ammunition to fire back at Believers. If you are an atheist or an agnostic then you have two options – put down the book now and find another way to spend your next few evenings, or read on in the hope that you will get at least two worthwhile benefits: 1. you will better understand the teaching of Jesus about the future and 2. you may acquire a better appreciation of normative biblical Christianity, especially as it concerns *the time*

---

3 In fact we might say their beliefs are not even "fringe"; rather they are *extra-Christian* beliefs. That is, they run on beyond normative Christian belief and into new areas.

of the end. That could just be of help to you – if you are genuinely confident of your atheist views, then why not read on?

Pigeon-hole

Your author [4] rejects in large part the varying [5] 'theologies' about the end time and the future. For the past 200 years differing 'theologies' have emerged that have been held by their adherents to represent a finality or a totality in terms of God's revelation and its correct interpretation. The adherents of such 'theologies' have often seemed more concerned to promote their own sectarian views rather than properly to understand and represent Jesus' on-going purposes and His clear directives about the future.

Not only does your author reject these various theologies, he largely rejects also their terminology and nomenclature. If then you, as a reader, were hoping that this book will support what may be your own 'pet' theology then you are likely to be disappointed – at least in that regard. We would, however, encourage you to persist with this book. At the least you will hopefully see from a different viewpoint what Jesus has said, and we trust (and pray) that you will be blessed anew as you do so. At best this book should help you clarify in your own mind what Jesus has said.

So this book resists being pigeon-holed into a particular category of theological 'understanding' or 'hermeneutic'. Rather, we seek to go back to Scripture to see what God has *clearly* set out, and also where God in His infinite wisdom has been *reticent* in the revealing that He provides. We repeat, God provides enough, neither too much nor too little, for us to prepare for, and to meet, what lies ahead.

Finally it must be said that there is also a question of timeliness: God has made it plain that some questions will be left until the end before they are fully clarified. In this we have in our mind, particularly, that passage from the prophet Jeremiah in its rather neat paraphrase in the *Good News Bible*: "**In days to come His people will understand this clearly**" (Jeremiah 23:20 and 30:24). At the very end, it seems, certain parts of the theological jigsaw will fall finally into place; until then we must trust where we cannot trace. The verse quoted above, we should add, is taken from chapter 23 in the context of false

---

4 This book is the result, in part, of informal discussions between a number of Christians over the period 2020-22. In the text of this book your author occasionally but deliberately uses the formulation "we" rather than "I" in expressing firm conclusions and opinions. This reflects areas where a number of other Believers have reached similar conclusions. It is not a "royal we"! Most of the views expressed and conclusions reached are by no means unique to this author.
5 and supposedly 'systematic' theologies

prophecy, where God is telling Jeremiah – and through him, the people of Israel – not to listen to false prophets. From verse 9 and again from verse 16, the clear instruction is to pay no attention to lying prophets. Although the whole chapter 23 of Jeremiah is alluding to a future return of the children of Israel from "all the countries" where God has banished them, in verse 20 the context will only be finally understood "in days to come".

In Jeremiah chapter 30 and verse 24, God is making a similar assertion. Israel will be restored (as it would be after the second, Babylonian, exile; and indeed also arguably after the third global dispersion pursuant to the Roman war culminating in AD70, which saw Israel leave the family of nations until May 1948) following its time of tribulation, but only after God's anger has been assuaged when He finally accomplishes the purposes of His heart. Then, and only then, in these "days to come" will we "understand this".

The pressing question right now is, quite simply, are we rapidly approaching those "days to come" in *our* today? Hopefully this book will provide confidence as we seek to address that crucial question. As we explore this, inevitably there will be associated or ancillary issues and questions. Whilst they are all relevant and vitally important, they are *out of scope* of this book. Essentially we hope to do justice to the issues on the left of our schematic below, but we will not address the questions on the right. We are sure readers will understand and agree that we must set clear parameters on this study:

IN SCOPE:

* Last Days
* End-Time prophecy of Ezekiel & Daniel
* Words of Jesus
* Second Coming
* Day of the Lord
* Revelation

RELATED BUT BROADLY OUT OF SCOPE FOR THIS BOOK:

* Last Judgment
* Bema seat
* Wrath of God
* Heaven / Hell
* Ezekiel 38-39 (Gog & Magog)

NOTE ON TEXT USAGE AND CONVENTIONS APPLIED

Readers will be helped by a short note on the choices your author has made regarding the capitalisation (or not) of terms used.

We aim for, and hope we have achieved, a broad consistency in this book. Since the Bible does not capitalise "last days" nor "end time" we avoid doing so, especially where we are quoting directly from the Scriptures. Where, however, we are speaking of that period in the world's history that is in the biblical sense the "last days", and as we have defined this in chapter 2, so we generally capitalise this as "Last Days", especially where in the context this usage helps to draw out this truth. In so doing readers thoughts are directed towards the truth that the last days is a well-worn biblical concept, and we argue in chapter 2 that this *defined* period in God's purposes will be "ended" at a point of His sovereign choosing.

The Bible nowhere speaks of "end times" (plural), yet it does speak of "the time of the end". The concept is obvious in a generic, even in a logical, sense. There must eventually be a time of an 'end' to this world preceding the creation of a new heaven and a new earth. Yet it is the end of *this present age* to which Scripture draws our attention, and the concept is first deployed in Daniel 8:17. Of interest, the editors of the old 1984 New International Version of the Bible, when incorporating an editor's heading atop Daniel chapter 12, use the capitalised term "The End Times". It is also true that many Christians speak almost incessantly about 'the end times' but with no clear definition of what they mean. This book, of course, aims to help clarify the matter. The *end time* really devolves down to a period immediately preceding Messiah Jesus' return to this world, a period otherwise characterised as a *great tribulation*, or as the late David Pawson used to say, "the big trouble". Generally speaking, where we refer to *that* time and where the context makes it useful, we capitalise it as "the End Time". But we do so sparingly.

As regards the "big trouble", where it helps to emphasise this truth, we capitalise as "Great Tribulation" or simply the Tribulation.

Gospel is capitalised when used as a specific reference to any or all of the four Gospels, Matthew, Mark, Luke, and John. Gospel in this book is lowercase when used as a general term meaning "good news", for example, "the gospel as presented in the New Testament," or "Paul took the gospel to the Romans".

Occasionally we use the term 'Believer' in preference to 'Christian' (a term that has a considerable array of potential meanings). Where we do so we generally capitalise it as "Believer". A Believer is someone who has believed "on" Jesus (in the sense of Acts 16:31) and received Him as Lord and as Saviour.

As salvation of the eternal soul (<u>from</u> condemnation and <u>to</u> eternal "tabernacling" (living) with God) is God's primary project for this world, it is not merely a "condition" of the soul, rather it is a statement of the eternal status of the true Believer. On that basis it is a 'proper noun' in our thinking, and so where suitable, it is capitalised as Salvation.

We use the term ekklesia in some places in preference to 'church'. We may also use the word 'assembly' in the same preference. But these words we do not capitalise. Similarly the word 'church' is generally not capitalised.

Antichrist is capitalised where it is referring to the individual (or person) that the Bible otherwise refers to as "the man of lawlessness" (2 Thessalonians 2:3). David Pawson used to make the relevant comment that the term 'antichrist' can equally be rendered as 'instead of Christ'. Any religion or belief system that elevates a person or a belief over and above Christ is in reality and practice 'instead of' Christ. So, for example, the popular western adoptee religion of Buddhism is very determinedly 'instead of Christ'. As an antichrist religion, however, it does not require capitalisation. All religions that decline to acknowledge Jesus as Lord – and that includes the 'religions' normatively known as Communism, Secularism and Fascism (etc) – are by the same token 'instead of Christ'.

Christ: wherever suitable we use the term Messiah in preference to Christ. "Christ" is essentially the anglicised/Greek translation of the Hebrew word "Massiasch" – or Messiah. Why not transliterate "Massiasch" into "Messiah"? It is more natural . . .

Special Note – throughout this book we use the English word *Jesus* and its Hebrew counterpart *Yeshua* interchangeably. More and more Christians are using the Lord's Hebrew name in everyday discourse, so this seems entirely appropriate. Some readers may be aware that certain commentators (particularly the useful One New Man Bible) use the phonetic Y'shua in preference to Yeshua. For clarity, the two words are the same; the first aims for a more phonetic Hebrew sound when read aloud. This book uses the normative Yeshua, as this has wide acceptance.

CHAPTER 1

TIMES AND SEASONS – GOD'S PERSPECTIVE

every teacher of the law who has become a disciple in the kingdom of heaven is like the owner of a house who brings out of his storeroom new treasures as well as old (Matthew 13: 52).

Meta-narrative of Scripture

Humans live within a time dimension, and God has given "times and seasons" for us as a part of His creation plan (Genesis 1: 14). To a human being, time is a problem – *eventually it must run out* – we are mortal! God operates outside our time-based limitations, but precisely how He does so is simply not for us to know. In a real sense, this is 'none of our business'.

God has graciously set in train a plan of Salvation; this plan is the entire and ultimate purpose for Mankind. God is building a family of those who place their trust in the finished work of Jesus achieved on The Cross. That is a huge and sweeping statement to make and this book is simply not the place to fully justify it[1]. God's Salvation plan is, however, the essential backdrop to the realty of times and seasons and indeed "last days" and "end times". We cannot ignore that God has an over-arching plan if we are to fully understand this reality about "last days" and how these "last days" reflect the Salvation plan.

As we first look at the 66 books that make up our canon of Scripture, we can sometimes be fazed at what seems to be the huge complexity of "the story". Your author argues that this apparent complexity is rather over-stated, things are not as complex as they may at first appear. In many ways God's Salvation plan is disarmingly simple.

The big story (meta-narrative) of the Bible is that God is building for Himself a family of those "called". To do this He reveals Himself and His purposes directly to all people, everywhere, who have the opportunity to respond to

---

1 There are hundreds if not thousands of books, films, blogs and graphics that explore illustrate this fully. We would recommend "The Eternal Purpose of God" by Lance Lambert and "Shalom – God's Master Plan" by Steve Maltz as helpful and readily available introductions. See also the "Further Reading" section at the back of this book.

Him. Those who respond positively are adopted into His family and will be with Him through eternity (when, incidentally, we shall be released from the earthly constraints of the time-dimension in which we presently live. Time is for now, it is not for later!). God has revealed Himself first through a People (the Hebrews, or "Jewish" people) and latterly through His Own Son, Yeshua (or 'Jesus' in English). God has revealed Himself in and through and throughout history. As is sometimes said, all history is ultimately His-Story. This meta-narrative contains lots of detail, numerous characters and many incidents, but they combine into a unified theme – the Salvation of all those who respond positively to God's overture of love and reconciliation through His Son.

Rejection of God's overture of love carries a negative consequence – that is, conscious separation from Him. Rejection of God's overture of love is not consequence-free (as some false teachers claim). When we live in rejection of God we are saying, in effect, that we think we ought to be "god" – or at least "god" over our own lives. In ultimately rejecting Him we finally and permanently get our wish and become a sort of "god", but a "god" over nothing, in a place of eternal separation. Soul-death or soul-extinction is not what God's Word reveals to us. Conscious separation from all that is good, noble, true and wholesome is what is prophesied for those who reject the most precious thing that God has ever given – His Own Son.

The "last days" that God's Word speaks of is the time when we have that opportunity to respond to God's overture of love. We will explore this more in Chapter 2.

God's meta-narrative reminds us, painfully, that Mankind chose to rebel against God [Genesis 3: 6]. This rebellion justified God's wonderful plan of salvation *which existed from before Creation* [John 17:24; Ephesians 1: 3-5; 1 Peter 1: 18-20; Titus 1: 1-2]. Mankind's rebellion simultaneously put into effect God's noble plan[2] that He would 'redeem' for Himself a *chosen people*, chosen and called out of this world and finding their security and purpose ("life") in His Kingdom. It is interesting to note that the "good news" that Jesus brought was not the good news that God loves you, nor was it the good news that you can be eternally forgiven for your sins. Nor was it, even, that Jesus is willing to die in your place as your substitute. No, the good news that Jesus brings is the good news of The Kingdom of Heaven:

---

2 God's 'noble plan' as we have described it was not His reaction to the Fall. It was His plan before time began.

From then on Jesus began to preach, "Repent, because the kingdom of heaven has come near." (Matthew 4:17). (Also Mark 1:15). In this Jesus was repeating what His cousin John (the baptist[3]) had already taught:

In those days John the Baptist came preaching in the wilderness of Judea, "Repent, for the kingdom of heaven is at hand." For this is he who was spoken of by the prophet Isaiah . . . (Matthew 3: 1-3)

The good news, then, is that The Kingdom - God's Kingdom - is near, so near that we can reach out and grab hold of it. It was true in Biblical times. It is still true today. We 'reach out and grab' deliberately and with determination: **Among those born of women there has not risen anyone greater than John the Baptist; yet he who is least in the kingdom of heaven is greater than he. From the days of John the Baptist until now, the kingdom of heaven has been forcefully advancing, and forceful men[4] lay hold of it** (Matthew 11:11-13 (NIV)).

Jesus is saying that to come fully into the Kingdom of Heaven requires deliberate, purposeful and determined action. Christians rightly understand this as meaning that - at a practical level - we receive Jesus as Lord and as Saviour, dedicating our ongoing lives to Him. This becomes a personal choice as we respond to the good news. So radical is the resulting change in our lives that Jesus describes it as being "born again".

God's meta-narrative might be described as taking on a recognisable 'shape'. The spiritual history of Mankind is measured and recorded through a Nation – indeed through a Chosen People. That Nation is the yardstick (or plumb-line) against which all other Nations shall be measured. Strangely, this is a plumb-line against which you and I shall also be measured!

From God's perspective (and from ours?) the "history" of the world begins at the Creation, when God created all. The Creation will in due time be supplanted by a New Creation. Betwixt these two points lies "history" as we perceive it. We might describe the New Creation as being "the end of history". We can plot the key twists and turns of our spiritual history in this way:

---

3 Many will point out that 'baptist' might better be translated as 'immerser'
4 'Men' is gender-neutral. It obviously includes women as well.

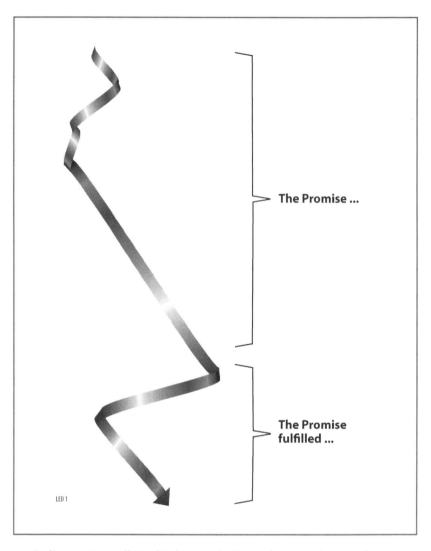

The Promise ...

The Promise
fulfilled ...

LED 1

God's promise to all Mankind is revealed in, and wrapped up in, what people tend to call "The Old Testament"[5]. The promise is finally worked-out or fulfilled in The New Testament, as God builds for Himself a People for His Own possession. The schematic above depicts a journey, but one that has several key spiritual turning points[6]. Perhaps readers may find this a helpful way of contemplating God's meta-narrative. Now we put some flesh on our schematic:

---

5 Sometimes called "Old Witness" or The Tanach.

6 In our schematic the twists and turns are depicted almost as a ribbon. That, in turn, reminds us of the idea of the so-called 'scarlet thread of redemption' that is said to run throughout Scripture, a seamless story with an interconnecting thread that is 'scarlet' as it anticipates the reality of the Saviour's blood shed for His people .....

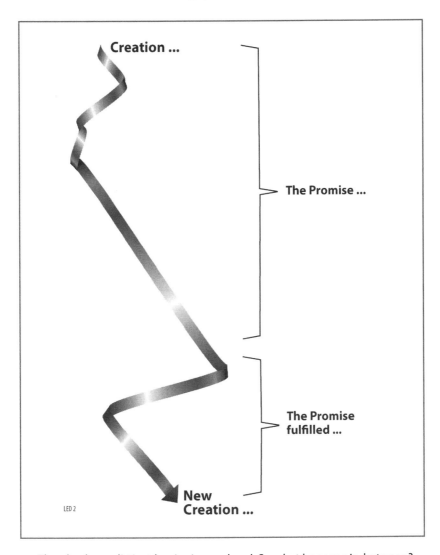

Creation ...

The Promise ...

The Promise
fulfilled ...

New
Creation ...

LED 2

The plan has a distinct beginning and end. So what happens in-between? Our next schematic sets this out. A few points need to be made. Firstly this is not drawn to scale, in any way! Secondly it is your author's viewpoint and other commentators might "see" the twists and turns differently. Thirdly the supporting Biblical quotations are the author's choice; others might illustrate with different Bible portions. Our schematic is not meant to be definitive:

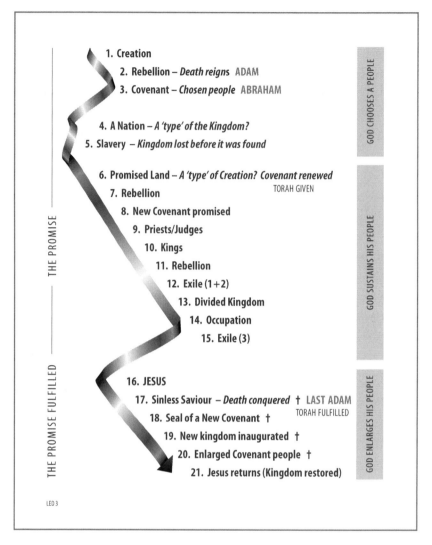

1. Creation
2. Rebellion – *Death reigns* ADAM
3. Covenant – *Chosen people* ABRAHAM

4. A Nation – *A 'type' of the Kingdom?*
5. Slavery – *Kingdom lost before it was found*

6. Promised Land – *A 'type' of Creation? Covenant renewed*
7. Rebellion   TORAH GIVEN
8. New Covenant promised
9. Priests/Judges
10. Kings
11. Rebellion
12. Exile (1+2)
13. Divided Kingdom
14. Occupation
15. Exile (3)

16. JESUS
17. Sinless Saviour – *Death conquered* † LAST ADAM
18. Seal of a New Covenant †   TORAH FULFILLED
19. New kingdom inaugurated †
20. Enlarged Covenant people †
21. Jesus returns (Kingdom restored)

GOD CHOOSES A PEOPLE

GOD SUSTAINS HIS PEOPLE

GOD ENLARGES HIS PEOPLE

THE PROMISE

THE PROMISE FULFILLED

LED 3

In the above we can see that God enters into a Covenant, first with Abraham and later with the Hebrew people as a whole. A geographically defined Land is allocated to this People (for all time![7]) but Israel loses possession of her Promised Land several times in her history, yet always with the promise of eventual restoration.

In this chapter and in this book we are not going to explore all 21 points in our schematic in detail, but at Appendix 5 interested readers will find suggested Bible passages that underscore this meta- narrative as we have

---

7 Strictly speaking, for all time up *until* the creation of a New Heaven and a New Earth (Revelation 21).

depicted it. Looking briefly at the above we see that during the Roman occupation of Judaea (point 14) Jesus was born. His entry to this world as the long-awaited and long-promised Messiah was the *final* major "turning point" in history, *when God became incarnate*. Death entered our world (point 2 above) when Mankind first rebelled – and, strictly speaking, it was Adam who rebelled, not Eve! Death was finally defeated by the Resurrection at Firstfruits (point 17 above) and God's new, expanded (or enlarged) Kingdom was inaugurated. Jesus will finally return to establish a combined new heaven and new earth, thus ending history as we understand it – and, we would add, terminating the Last Days as we have defined it in this book.

Times and Seasons

In God's plan there are distinct or discrete times. Some theologians refer to these times *as they see them* as 'dispensations'. In turn, this leads on to something called dispensational theology. "Dispensationalism" as a theological construct is not a schema that this author holds to. Whilst I consider that dispensational theology can be a useful framework for understanding God's over-arching purposes, and in that sense has a certain value, yet I do not see that this theology is clearly taught in Scripture itself [8]. I argue that it is derived principally from eisegesis rather than from textual exegesis – that is from *reading-into* Scripture something that one may wish to find there, rather than *reading-out of* Scripture what is clearly revealed.

And yet . . . The idea that there are discrete periods wherein God works out a particular purpose is at least suggested by Scripture, and we have picked-up on that thought in our schematics above. So we must be reticent and gentle as we reject Dispensationalism at the very same time that we suggest viewing history in the sense of times and seasons. The key difference, perhaps, is that we do not proffer our schematic as set in 'tablets of stone' or as a 'systematic theology': rather ours is a simple framework to assist comprehension. Your author trusts that our Bible references (Appendix 5) tend to support and not undermine what we are suggesting. Readers can make up their own minds . . .

Ecclesiastes chapter 3 certainly suggests that there are "times" within which certain things are right and proper and, dare we say it, justifiable. The Lord Jesus Himself spoke in terms of eras. He spoke of *signs* of the end and of things happening "in those days" and "at that time". Jesus criticised the crowd

---

8 David Pawson in his helpful short book "Defending Christian Zionism", includes an interesting brief section on the history and development of dispensational theory. The doctrine did not emerge as a "school" until the 1830s.

for its inability to understand the season in which they were living, when the Son of God was with them in the flesh (Luke 12: 56a). Do we understand the season we are living in today, and will Jesus criticise us for our slowness to see, as it were, the writing on the wall?! In Luke chapter 22 Jesus spells out signs of the end of the present age, for which signs we are to keep open, figuratively, a *weather eye* – we are to look out for these signs actually happening. Jesus pointed towards the future, when all things will be put to rights (John 16:22-23). So Jesus also recognised times and seasons.

Finally, in Jesus' revelation of the future to the apostle John, whilst John was on the island of Patmos (Revelation 1:9), there are many allusions to the future age(s) of Mankind. Whether these are literal, metaphorical or given in strict chronological order (these things are widely debated), Revelation still gives the firm impression that there are discrete eras through which God works out His purposes.

God's perspective, if we may reverently state it thus, is that within the times that He has ordained, and of which He is in total control, He is working out a definite purpose. Jesus is, after all, the alpha and omega, the beginning and the end (Revelation 22:13). Furthermore God knows the end from the beginning (Isaiah 46:10) and He has graciously revealed key elements of His purposes to the eyes of the Believer. What is amazing, perhaps, is that God has not left us in the dark. Rather He has entrusted us with certain sacred truths, in which we are to place our trust. We do not fear the future because we know Who holds the future. Let us conclude this chapter with a short portion from Isaiah 46:

Remember this and be brave;
take it to heart, you transgressors!
Remember what happened long ago,
for I am God, and there is no other.
I am God, and no one is like me.
I declare the end from the beginning,
and from long ago what is not yet done,
saying: my plan will take place,
and I will do all my will.
I call a bird of prey from the east,
a man for my purpose from a far country.
Yes, I have spoken; so I will also bring it about.
I have planned it; I will also do it.
Listen to me, you hardhearted,
far removed from justice:
I am bringing my justice near;
it is not far away,
and my salvation will not delay.
I will put salvation in Zion,
my splendour in Israel.

Praise the Lord, indeed!

CHAPTER 2

THE LAST DAYS

the anger of the LORD will not turn back until He has performed and carried out the purposes of His heart. In the last days you will clearly understand it (Jeremiah 23:20 and 30:24).

Last and End

As suggested in the previous chapter Christians have, at various times down through history, rightly and logically asked the rhetorical yet highly practical question, *"are we now living in the final days?"* In each era, as appalling circumstances have so often conspired, and as these circumstances seem to have "matched" to greater or lesser extent the 'signs' that Jesus in particular spoke of, so it has been necessary to ask ourselves, *just how close are we to the end –* specifically, how close are we to the bodily return of Messiah Jesus to this world?

In later pages we will explore what the return of Jesus may mean in and to this world, noting that there are varying and competing 'understandings' of this matter amongst Christians, some of which are mutually exclusive in outcome. For now, we restrict our investigation to understanding two key ideas – there are "last days" and there are "end times", but are they the same? Confusion about these two simple ideas has lain at the heart of the development of varying schools of "theology" which are themselves *wide of the mark* in terms of what the Bible straightforwardly teaches.

No wonder that confusion reigns, and *angst* and *argument* are the two 'un-love children' of such competing ideas. It really does not have to be so complex! What Jesus gave us in His teaching, and what God has given us through His Word, inspired by His Spirit, is fully comprehensible to ordinary faithful people. That is not to say that these things are necessarily 'easy', yet the Scriptures were given for ordinary people and written in the common language of the ordinary man and woman. So we must assume that these truths are *for the many* and not the reserve of the 'few' who may see themselves somehow as 'specialists', as theologians or as 'clergy'. God speaks plainly to all people . . .

'Last days' is a term used in many places in Scripture to describe the final phase of this world in its present guise. In The Tanach the last days are anticipated as the age of Messianic fulfillment (Isaiah 2:2 ; Micah 4:1). The New Testament writers understand themselves to be living in the Last Days, which they see as the era of the gospel, the good news of Jesus. We would comment, in passing, that "Dipensationalists" understand the world to exist in seven distinct timeframes (or "dispensations"). In their view the present era is the "Christian" dispensation, or *the church age*. As authors we consider that the ideas of Dispensationalism, whilst a useful framework of understanding, are not ultimately biblical *in the sense they are not clearly and unequivocally taught by Scripture*. Dispensationalism, then, is not in the same category of understanding as, for example, the Resurrection of Jesus. We would argue that Dispensationalism is the product of a largely eisegetical[1] hermeneutic, not an exegetical[2] hermeneutic.

As this point some readers may be discombobulated by the sudden appearance of 'technical' theological terms. Having just written that what God has graciously given is straightforward to understand (at least in principle) we are immediately apologising for introducing some complex ideas! A person's over-arching hermeneutic[3], then, will govern the way that they approach Scripture. Your author believes that an exegetical hermeneutic is the safest and surest way to engage with the Scriptures, and believes un-abashedly, it is the way that God principally intends His Word to be understood. So we must attempt first to read *out of* Scripture what the biblical writer evidently intends to express, and only dig deeper or more speculatively where the text or the context clearly suggest that other signals for interpretation are being given.

Our first line of defence here must be to state that Dispensationalism, in its complexity and in its normative forms, is not *clearly* taught in Scripture. So whatever complexity (and confusion) that may have arisen *via this route*[4], it is not the fault of the Bible! Nor by extension, if we may say this reverently, is it the fault of the Holy Spirit, either. Ultimately it is the fault of 'theologians', howsoever that term may be understood. Having stated clearly that we are not Dispensationalists, your authors will add for clarity we are not hostile to the

---

1 Reading into to Scripture what you expect, or want, to find. Making the text "fit" the theory? [eis = into]

2 Reading out of Scripture what is plainly taught and exploring its ancient and contemporary implications, thus allowing the text to speak plainly. [ex = out of]

3 Theory and methodology of interpretation, especially the interpretation of biblical texts. Note that God gave ordinary people straightforward texts, by and large. We are not so much called to "interpret" texts, as to live by what the Bible plainly teaches. Yet a certain degree of interpretation will be necessary, especially for the more challenging passages and where "types" and "shadows" are being used within the text.

4 There are indeed many other routes to confusion!

concepts encapsulated within this 'theology'. We repeat that Dispensational ideas can provide a useful framework to describe God's purposes, but the key language and concepts employed by Dispensationalists are very often extra-Scriptural (not in the Bible!). The late David Pawson, in his book "Defending Christian Zionism", provides a helpful brief outline of the origins of Dispensationalism. We recommend his chapter 1 in this regard. Pawson's book is a useful resource at many levels (see further reading section) and helps to set out in simple terms why many Christians understand Israel to have a distinct and continuing purpose throughout the *last days*, and indeed in the *end time*. But this understanding in no way depends upon Dispensationalism (Pawson was not a Dispensationalist).

Whilst rejecting Dispensationalism's seven separate periods as being the only, or primary, way to understand God's over-arching purposes, yet we acknowledge the concept of a *church age*, being that period *from* the outpouring of the Holy Spirit at Pentecost *until* the return of Christ to this world. Author Peter Sammons explored this in his earlier book "The Messiah Pattern" (2018) where he used the schematic below to illustrate, conceptually, a model that is useful and defendable by direct reference to Scripture:

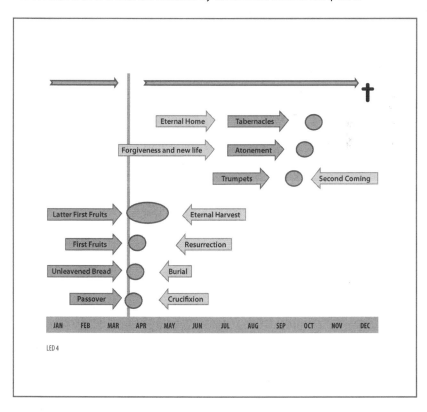

LED 4

In the schematic above we see illustrated in time-order the seven Biblical feasts of Leviticus chapter 23 and how they prefigure the work of Messiah Jesus – these feasts are in fact *shadows*[5] of the Messiah. In 'Christological' terms, the first three of these feasts have occurred and lie in the past, the fourth is happening now, and the final three lie in the future. On this basis we can represent our current era as "the church age"[6] in this way:

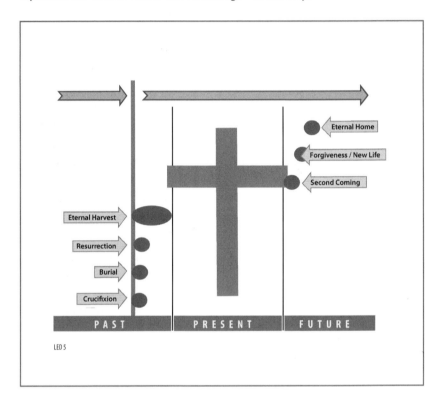

As we are about to discover, the present era (or the church age) can also be understood to be '*the last days*'.

---

5 Author Simon Pease is progressively developing teaching material on the types and shadows of Messiah. These types and shadows are a wonderful affirmation of the interconnectedness of Scripture and the dependability of God's out-working purposes. Types and shadows give us confidence, not confusion . See further reading section at the back of this book.

6 We do of course recognise there are some serious objections to this term 'church age'. However at this point we are opting for straightforwardness and simply depicting these ideas in 'broad brush strokes'. We hope readers will appreciate the necessity for this. Readers are, of course, encouraged to study the Biblical feasts as a separate, but linked, theme to this book and its focus on *The Last Days*. Peter Sammons' earlier book will be found to be a useful starting point for separate reflection.

In these last days

The apostle Peter explained that the events of the day of Pentecost (rendered as *Latter First Fruits* in our schematic above) are the fulfilment of Joel 2:28 – "**this is what was spoken by the prophet Joel: And in the last days it shall be, God declares, that I will pour out my Spirit upon all flesh**"(Acts 2:16-17). The author of the letter to the Hebrews states that God "**spoke of old to our fathers by the prophets; but in these last days He has spoken to us by His Son**" (Hebrews 1: 1-2). The last days, then, are days of gospel blessing in which *the gift of Life*, procured for all people by Jesus through His perfect life, sacrificial death, resurrection and glorification, is freely available throughout the world. There is literally no reason why any person should live life in ignorance of Jesus. These *last days* are, therefore, the days of opportunity for unbelievers to repent and turn to God. By the same token they are the days when the Believer must be proclaiming the gospel message throughout the world. That is our primary task, or our *prime directive*, to use a modern term.

It should also be observed that the *last days* are a period of testing for the disciples of Jesus (that is, for true Christians). We are called to faithful perseverance in the face of hostility and contempt displayed by the ungodly. The apostle Paul warned Timothy that "**in the last days will come times of stress**" (2 Timothy 3:1). Peter similarly warned that "**scoffers will come in the last days**" (2 Peter 3:3). The short letter of Jude states: "**remember, beloved, the predictions of the apostles of our Lord Jesus Christ; they said to you "in the last time there will be scoffers, following their own ungodly passions"**" (Jude 18).

The Baker Encyclopedia of the Bible (1988 volume 3, page 1310) reminds us:

> "for those who persist in their ungodliness, indeed, these are literally their last days. However prosperous they may appear to be at present, there is no glorious future for them. "You have laid up treasures for the last days", James ironically warns those who are intent on amassing for themselves earthly riches (James 5:3). So also our Lord gave the solemn warning that "a man's life does not consist in the abundance of his possessions", calling that person a fool who lays up treasures for himself, but who is not rich towards God (Luke 12: 15-21)".

The Baker Encyclopedia might have added that Jesus also tells us to store up for ourselves treasures in heaven (Matthew 6: 19-21). Given that the days in which we presently live are the *last days* rather than the penultimate days, we might add that this understanding of God's outworking of the *last days* (which is emphasised in both the Old Testament and the New) rather undermines any 'theology' of universalism[7]. If the unrepentant can be "saved" beyond these *last days*, then surely the Bible would have called these days in which we presently live the 'penultimate days', so indicating a further and future 'opportunity' to get right with God? But no, our era is definitively the *last* days.

Jude 18 furthermore highlights that the idea of the last days is also conveyed by other similar terms such as the "last time". This is illustrated in 1 Peter 1:20 where we read that Messiah Jesus was "**destined before the foundation of the world but was made manifest at the end of the times**", which is generally understood to be in the final stages of the history of Mankind in this world. The plural "last days" gives the impression of a period of some duration – elsewhere Jesus Himself spoke of a land-owner who goes away for a long period of time (Luke 20: 9 – the parable of the vineyard owner). The correctness of this impression of an *extended* period is underscored by the reality that it has now been nearly 2000 years since the ascension of Messiah Jesus, Who has left His Spirit to indwell us in the absence of His physical proximity here with us.

In every generation the end of this (final) age is always imminent, and so John describes this time as "**the last hour**" (1 John 2:18). Down through each era of history there have been many apparent "signs" of which Jesus warned, and there have certainly been many antichrist figures in many places in this world, whom have seemed (at least locally) to "fit" the evil genius of that figure whom the Bible tells us is yet to come at the End Time. On that basis, the struggle of Christians to understand in each era current political and societal affairs (and their spiritual 'drivers') has been entirely rational, but in each case hitherto has tried to understand these things with one significant piece of the 'spiritual jigsaw puzzle' missing. That missing piece has always been Israel (see chapter 4 for more on this). Whilst some scoffers deride previous generations for their fixation on the idea of 'the End Time' and their sometimes spectacular errors in 'prophecy', as authors we do not condemn previous generations for their wrestling with this question, but we repeat that *previous generations have struggled to understand with clarity because of their lack of insight into God's purposes in and around Israel*. These purposes were arguably thrown into sharp relief in May 1948, at least for those with spiritual eyes to see.

The apostle John states: "**many antichrists have come, therefore we know this is the last hour**" (1 John 2:18). We repeat, the *end* of these last days (a key focus of our thesis in this book) is always at imminent hand for

---

7   A belief that all are saved for eternity

each generation. One day that time will emerge in reality for a particular generation and, because of this, there is a need for constant vigilance, which Jesus specifically commanded and for which He commended His followers. Furthermore, Jesus stated that that we do not know the day or the hour (but note carefully, He did not leave this question entirely in the shadows) when He will return, and so we are to be ready for His return at all times (Matthew chapters 24 and 25 unveil Jesus' instructions in this regard).

End

Whilst the concept of The Last Days is encountered throughout The Tanach and the New Testament, the concept of *the end* is also found, but with lower frequency. For readers with a reasonably detailed Bible Concordance, a word-search on the word 'end' will quickly and easily yield valuable insights. For the moment we will concentrate our thoughts on just four Bible references. In doing so we do not want to be found guilty of the cardinal sin of taking a verse out of context to 'prove' a point! These four are merely illustrative, and we expect to re-engage with each later in this book in a more thorough way. For the time being, however:

a) Daniel 12:9 – **go your way Daniel because the words are closed up and sealed until the time of the end** . . .

The book of Daniel deals extensively with the concept of the very end. In the verse above, we simply note two things: (1) there will be an end and (2) that certain key questions will be "sealed" away from our full understanding until the end. It is to be expected, then, that at the end there will be a widespread outpouring of Holy Spirit to enable us to fully comprehend many mysteries that have baffled previous generations of believers. God in His wisdom will reserve special understanding for that final generation.

b) Rev 21:6 and 22:13 – **I Am the alpha and omega, the beginning and the end** . . .

Here we encounter the simple fact that Jesus is the beginning as well as the end. More and more Christians are becoming aware of, and are rightly excited by, the fact that Jesus is found on every page of the Bible. Hebrew scholars point out that in the very first word of the bible = beresheit (literally, *in-beginning*, a single word in Old Testament Hebrew) the mission and accomplishment of Jesus is encoded, like spiritual DNA. [Literally in the picture language of Hebrew, and letter by letter, this spells out from right to left Son-God-Destroyed-Own Hand-Cross.] This matter of the opening words of the Bible and how they speak of Jesus must await a separate book (which we are sure will come!) but it is fascinating that in these latter days – and we use that term advisedly – ordinary Christians are rediscovering wonderful truths that have lain buried (by 'theology'?!) for nigh on twenty centuries. Are we seeing Daniel 12:9 being worked-out in our own generation? Readers must make up their own minds . . .

But in the light of the first word of the Bible (above) we can say with absolute assurance that Jesus is both the beginning and the end. So the end for the believer is . . . Jesus. Incidentally, in Isaiah 44:6 God has already affirmed that He is *the first and the last*. So this is another affirmation of the deity of Messiah Jesus[8]. Let us remind ourselves what is the last word of the Bible . . . Readers can check this for themselves if they do not already know!

c) Matthew 24:6, Mark 13-7, Luke 21-9 – "**such things must happen but the end is still to come**"

Jesus taught about the very end, plainly with the intention that His followers will read, mark, learn, inwardly digest and live by these truths. If Jesus has given us this information (and He has) then it is for our blessings and it is needful for us. But in Jesus' statement, captured by three of the four gospel writers, the Lord affirms there will be an *end* which will terminate these last days. That is the simple lesson we want to impart here.

d) 1 Peter 4:7 – "**the end of all things is near**"

This first letter of Peter is addressed to God's elect (1 Peter 1:1), that is, to everyone who is a true follower of Jesus and is saved by Him. We might say, Peter's letter has *your* name on it if you are a disciple of Jesus. Peter's choice of those words "the end" indicates that he sees that Jesus' return is imminent, an idea we explored earlier in this chapter. Peter simply underscores the point.

The last day

At this point we hope readers are gaining some purchase on the idea that *the last days* are the days of the New Covenant. This again is a huge subject and awaits its own separate book! If the era of the New Covenant is simultaneously the era of the church, or *the church age*, then our task now is simply to make a clear and 'operational' distinction between the *last days* (that shall be finally terminated by the *end time*) and the *end time*. 'End time' is hardly used in Scripture, but the concept is clearly there and the remainder of this book seeks to explore it in terms of the interconnectedness of Old and New Testament prophecy about this culmination of God's purposes.

---

8 A recent and powerful book exploring the deity of Jesus is David Lambourn's "But is He God?". See further reading section at the end of this book for details.

The *last days* will be terminated by . . . the last day! The use of the term "day" in the singular reminds us of the New Testament concept of the "day of the Lord" which is used so often in The Tanach. In the Old Testament the day of the Lord is often presented as an awful day of final judgment against rebellious man – specifically, those who are unrepentant – but with the implication that it is simultaneously the day of salvation and vindication of God's people (e.g. Isaiah 2:12-22; Ezekiel 13:5; Joel 1:15; 2: 1,11; Amos 5:18-24; Zephaniah 1:7, 14).

The climax of history will be **"the day of the Lord"** which will occur suddenly (1 Thessalonians 5:2). This last of the last days will be the day of final judgment of those who have rejected the good news of Salvation through Jesus. As The Baker Encyclopedia of the Bible, volume 3 reminds us[9], it will simultaneously be the time of purification of this present 'fallen' world and the restoration of the created order, so that in the new heaven and the new earth all God's purposes in creation are brought to fulfillment: *"Then at the consummation of our redemption, at last fully conformed to our Redeemer's likeness, we shall enter into the enjoyment of His eternal glory"* says The Baker Encyclopedia. (See 1 John 3: 2; also Romans 8: 19-25; Revelation 21: 1-8).

Christians are reminded by the apostle Paul that on this last day, which he refers to simply as **"that day"**, the value of our building upon the one foundation (Messiah Jesus) will be fully revealed. What we have done with our lives will be known. It is helpful to note at this point that it is not the security of our Salvation in Messiah Jesus that is in any way "at stake" here; rather it is to assess the extent to which we can meet Jesus with joy and confidence, or bluntly with shame, at His coming (2 John 2:28). Each man's work will become manifest as Paul asserts: **"for the Day will disclose it . . . if the work which any man has built on the foundations survives, he will receive a reward. If any man's work is burned up, he will suffer loss, though he himself will be saved"** (1 Corinthians 3: 13-15). This is a hugely important truth for us to engage with.

We are indebted to The Baker Encyclopedia[10] Volume 3 for these final thoughts which are summarised from its entry on the **Last Days**:

The Last Days are followed by the everlasting day of Messiah's kingdom when God will be all in all (Philippians 3: 20-21; 1 Corinthians 15: 28). The last day is also the day of triumph and resurrection, when Messiah has promised to raise up everyone who believes on Him (John 6: 39,40,44,54). The Last Days are like night compared with the glory that will be revealed at Messiah's return, so that the end of these Last Days will also be the beginning of God's unending day.

---

9 Page 1311
10 See further reading section at the end of this book

So we have Paul's encouragement to the believers in Rome: "**It is full time now for you to awake from sleep. For salvation is nearer to us now than when we first believed. The night is gone. The day is at hand. Let us therefore cast off the works of darkness and put on the armour of light**" (Romans 13:11-12). The realisation that we are in the Last Days and that *the final day* is approaching ought to have a powerful effect on the quality and intensity of our living in the here and now. "**What sort of persons ought you to be in lives of holiness and godliness waiting for and hastening the coming of the day of God?**" Peter exclaims, adding that in the light of these last days we should be "**zealous to be found in our Lord without spot or blemish, and at peace**" (2 Peter 3: 11-14).

Chapter Summary

It is to be hoped that readers will now have more confidence in the clear distinction between The Last Days and The End Time. After the time of Jesus in His first incarnation everything changed – forever. He inaugurated what people now call the New Covenant (sometimes rendered in theological discourse, interestingly, as the *renewed* covenant, which your author considers to be a helpful perspective) and Jesus is now working in His harvesting season which will persist until His family is complete and He returns again, as bridegroom, to claim His bride.

Where in the past confusion has reigned over *when the end is to come*, we suggest that part of the confusion is explained by our failure to understand that the *last days* have persisted since the ascension. Once this nuance is well understood, many references across Scripture take on a different hue. Furthermore the time of the end is seen more distinctly and separately. At the risk of stating the obvious, the terms 'Last Days' and 'End Times' are used interchangeably amongst at least some Bible expositors, which tends towards mistaken expectations, if not outright confusion.

In his letter to the Corinthian church, apostle Paul opens his tenth chapter with a clear 'warning' from Israel's past, stating that Israel was punished by God directly for its rebellion against Him. This history, says Paul, serves as a warning to the disciples of Jesus too. In verse 11 Paul says: "**these things happened to them as examples that were written down as warnings for us, on whom the fulfillment of the ages has come**" (1 Corinthians 10: 11). Paul clearly sees the fulfillment as already here, so the next key task on God's salvific agenda is the return of His Son Jesus as Lord in what many understand will be His 'millennial rule'[11]. Whilst the term *millennial rule* is not specifically used in Scripture, nevertheless, this understanding is a reasonable exegesis of various texts. The fulfilment of the ages has come but the final outworking of this lies still in our future.

Jesus has triumphed over sin and death. Salvation is available today for all who trust in Jesus' achievement on the Cross. That is the 'fulfilment' of the ages and marked the beginning of a final harvesting period. That harvesting shall persist until Jesus' family is complete.

Praise God indeed!

---

11   See our chapter 13.

CHAPTER 3

THE END TIMES

the vision is yet for the appointed time;
it hurries toward the goal and it will not fail.
Though it delays, wait for it; for it will certainly come.
It will not delay long **(Habakkuk 2:3).**

The church age?

If *last days* are well aired across Scripture, the specific term 'end time' is noticeable by its absence. And so we must be cautious in using the term – and possibly be careful to explain precisely what we mean when we do use it. The first significant use of the term "end" is where God tells Noah that He will make an end to prediluvian[1] Mankind (Genesis 6:13). That was a previous era to ours and plainly does not refer to things that still lie in our future. Yet *the flood* does remind us that in God's economy there are times and seasons and that God does periodically 're-set' the clock as new eras are entered into, by ending definitively the preceding era.

It is in the book of Daniel, which plainly *does* deal with end-time issues, that we encounter this specific term (i.e. Daniel 12:4). We shall not try to unravel the difficulties of Daniel, Zechariah, and Ezekiel here, nor how they "mesh" with themes developed in the book of Revelation. In this chapter we simply try to clarify the distinction between *last days*, and *end times*. Many modern translations of the Bible, where their editors introduce section headings within passages, will head-up Daniel chapter 12 as 'a prophecy of the end times'. Chapter 12 plainly speaks of a time when God's judgment is executed *across* this planet. But immediately having given this glimpse into the future, Daniel is told that the meaning of the prophecy is to be 'sealed' until the end. No wonder, then, that the 'church' has struggled to understand Daniel and other matters pertaining to the End over the past nineteen hundred years! God has made it obscure until the End (or near to the end). Our question today, as in every previous era, remains 'how close are we to the end?' It is suggested

---

1 before the flood of Genesis chapters 6 to 8

that there are strong grounds for assuming that, today, we are in the "final approach" phase – to borrow an aeronautical term – that we are within sight of the end. In this assumption we are far from alone, may Christians have reached a similar conclusion. Your author is not, however, dogmatic about this matter, but merely confirms here that this is his considered view for reasons broadly expressed throughout this book.

In Revelation chapters 21 and 22 at the very end of our Bible, Jesus describes Himself as **the beginning and the end** (Rev 21:16 and 22:13). In our previous chapter of this book, we noted that the purpose of Jesus is set out in the very first word of the Bible – beresheit – literally in English "in-beginning". And of course Jesus is at the very end of Revelation too. Everything in the Bible is about the Lord Jesus – or more correctly *Yeshua ha Massiasch* – Jesus the Messiah in English. Jesus is 'hidden in plain sight' in the first word of the Bible. He is the last word of the Bible, and arguably He is everything else in-between.

Yeshua Himself spoke about the end of "this age" (Matthew 13: 40, 49). Embedded within Jesus' teaching is the idea that there will be an end, following which we shall all be held accountable. So Yeshua speaks in Matthew chapters 24 and 25 plainly and directly about signs that the End is drawing near. And in Matthew 28: 20 we have His wonderful promise that He will be with us all, at all times, "**to the very end of the age**".

We shall look shortly at Yeshua's direct teaching about the end times. Right now we reflect once again on the question what is "the age" of which Jesus speaks in Matthew 28: 20? What is the age that shall have an "end"? There are a number of helpful ways of answering this question. Some will say simply that this age is "the church age". In one sense this is correct, but in another, it is somewhat questionable! Some say that the 'church' was born at Pentecost[2] as the Holy Spirit was then outpoured upon all Believers in God's new and liberal way. It is certainly helpful to think of our present era from this perspective except that this manner of thinking has the unintended, and subtle, consequence that we move progressively into the reality of 'churchianity' and of the church as a human institution – and even as a societal 'estate' alongside the King and the Law. These are problematic outcomes! For a moment, however, let us persist with this idea of *the church age* and glean from it what is helpful.

In my book "The Messiah Pattern" I explore the theme of the "rhythm" of our Christian worshipful year through the Hebrew *biblical feasts*, each of which speaks indirectly about the life, mission, ministry and achievement of Jesus – themes that are 'hidden in plain sight'. There are in fact *seven* biblical feasts. In

---

2 That is, the New Testament church. In the LXX the Old Testament *assembly* (or *congregation*) is frequently rendered as 'church' – a helpful perspective, we think.

Christological terms three lie in our past, three lie in our future and one is our present-day situation. The diagrams below illustrate this visually.

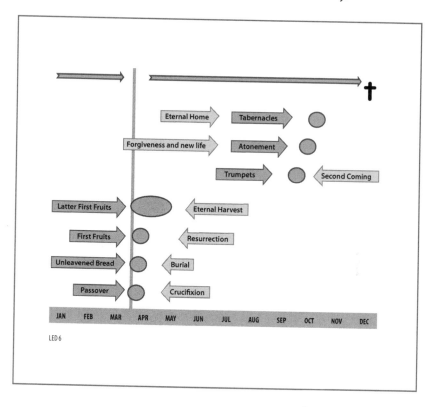

LED 6

In the above diagram we see the seven 'feasts' with their ancient title and their present Christological significance. These 'feasts' are, in order, and using plain English functional names: Passover, Unleavened Bread, First Fruits, Latter First Fruits (perhaps better described by its Hebrew name Shavuot), Trumpets, Atonement and Tabernacles. We will not over-burden this book with what must be a separate study[3], but suffice to say that these biblical feasts (collectively *moedim*, and singularly *moed*) represent *prophetically* the life, mission, ministry, death, resurrection and future triumph of the Lord Yeshua. Seen schematically, as above, they impress in our mind's eye God's over-arching plan at its simplest.

Recognising that of these seven moed events, three lie in the past, three yet in the future and one is our time today, so we can with a degree of legitimacy refer to this present era as *the church age* (which must, in its own turn, come to an end). Re-casting the schematic somewhat we can depict the eras from our

---

3 *The Messiah Pattern* is published by Christian Publications International (CPI). At time of writing this book it is also freely available as a PDF on the CPI website.

present perspective in this way:

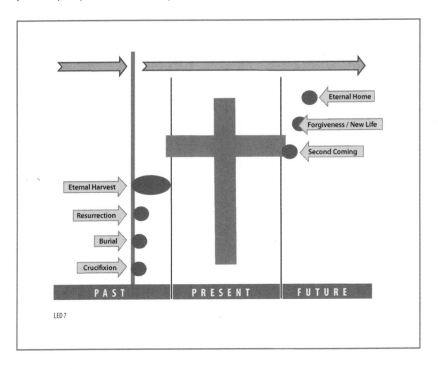

LED 7

The first three events lie in the past. The fourth is our present situation today. The period of Latter First Fruits (Shavuot/Pentecost), although celebrated in the late spring, persists throughout the hot summer months until the whole harvest is gathered in. For 'the church' today this is the era of preaching the gospel and extending the Kingdom until Christ returns, at the end of the age.

We should not get side-tracked into too many separate themes, but we do need gently to challenge the idea that we should think of our present era as "the church age". Whilst in one sense the idea is helpful as a 'short-hand' way of thinking about God's purposes, in another it is actually damaging and counter-productive. Firstly, there is the inconvenient fact that strictly speaking, the word 'church' is not found in our Bibles, nor are people called into 'the church'. Jesus preached the good news, not of the 'church' but of the Kingdom! Our task is to draw people into God's Kingdom, not into 'the church'. We shall not attempt to resolve this awkward question here. But we will allow an interesting glossary term from the One New Man Bible (ONMB) to reveal the contours of this debate:

Congregation is the appropriate translation of the Greek word Ekklesia, which means a group of people who have gathered for some particular purpose. Although often translated church, no Greek word meaning 'church' is used in the Greek New Testament. Another Greek word sometimes translated 'church', in James 2:2, is Sunagoga, now written synagogue in English. Sunagoga means a gathering of people or an assembly. Church is not an appropriate translation of either word because that in our minds refers to an organisation or to a building, while both Greek words, Ekklesia and Sunagoga, refer to people. The people are far more important than the organisation or the building! Therefore in this translation Ekklesia is always translated congregation, and Sunagoga is translated synagogue or public gathering. Ekklesia is also used in the Septuagint, the Greek translation of the Hebrew Scriptures, where it is translated congregation. Since the authors of the Bible did not use a word for 'church', the word 'church' does not appear in the Scripture of this ONMB volume.

The editor of the ONMB makes a helpful and serious point. Some Christians indeed avoid the word 'church' for this very reason. 'Congregation' or 'assembly' are arguably better terms to use as they avoid the World's popular assumption that 'the church' is a hierarchy, an institution and a power structure comprising clergy and laity (or should that be clergy *versus* laity?). This is not a 'model' that Jesus would recognise. In reality 'the church' is all those who assemble before God to worship Him and to declare their allegiance to Him. So we are God's assembly of those called-out from this world and into His Kingdom. This *calling out* is so radical, that Jesus reminds us we are to store up for ourselves treasures in heaven and not here on earth. Friendship with this world is enmity towards God (James 4: 4), which implies we are to see ourselves principally in God's Kingdom and locate our true citizenship there, not here. Rather than being citizens here, we are ambassadors here of God's Kingdom (2 Corinthians 5: 20).

These ideas mean we should be cautious – in fact very cautious – in using the term 'church'. Ideally we should use the term 'congregation' or even 'assembly' as these better describe who we are and how we relate to our Saviour. Furthermore, the idea of a congregation (that is, those who congregate) implies the congruent idea that Christians are ambassadors, here, and part of our role as ambassadors is proactively to assemble before our King, to worship Him and to underscore (in the eyes of this World) our primary allegiance to Him.

A surfeit of prophets?

There are four biblical books that give deep insight into *the end time*. These are Daniel, Zechariah and Ezekiel from the Tanach, and Revelation from the New Testament. In our next chapter we shall explore a little the interconnectedness of these prophetic messages, but for now will simply note that each raises aspects of *the end time*, and it is profitable to keep in view all four (together with other scriptures) as we try to reach conclusions about what these Spirit-inspired revelations are telling us today. As we approach the Bible, particularly the Tanach, it can seem a daunting exercise particularly as we encounter prophet after prophet, who collectively seem to be delivering similar messages about Israel's serial sin followed inevitably by God's judgment. These can, in our minds, all blur confusingly into one . . .

It is helpful to bear in mind the broad sweep of biblical history and how individual biblical prophets (and some narratives) reflect that big picture. In brief, Israel was granted its *Promised Land* by God, but was told that living there in peace and security would be wholly dependent on their obeying the terms of the Covenant (the Abraham Covenant, later renewed and extended in the time of Moses). Disobey, and there would be consequences . . . In Israel's history there have been three great exiles from the Promised Land, pursuant to Israel's serial rebellions against God's core commands. The first when 'Israel' (the ten tribes to the North of the Promised Land) was defeated and captured by Assyria, and taken into exile. These ten tribes never returned and are often referred to as the 'lost tribes of Israel'. The second was essentially the same cause and outcome when 'Judah' was captured by Babylon. From this second exile there was a return of a 'remnant'. The third was the far more prolonged exile[4] from the lands (that were by then mere backwater provinces in the Roman Empire), imposed by the Romans after Israel's rebellion culminating in AD70 as Jerusalem was sacked by Rome. Christians understand that God's intention was always that the Promised Land would ultimately be restored, and that this prophetic truth took on practical shape in May 1948 when the State of Israel was (re)born.[5]

That is the big picture. But from the viewpoint of non-expert Bible readers the interplay between these events is not easy to follow. (In fact the third exile (diaspora) at the hand of Rome *was* indirectly prophesied but not stated as such in the canon of New Testament Scripture, which essentially closed with that first Christian generation and the gospel beginning to go global, *before* AD70). It is

---

4 Technically, the post-Roman diaspora
5 This view generally is disputed by Liberal Christians i.e. those that do not hold to the inerrancy nor literalness of Scripture. They see the return of Israel as an historical aberration . . .

hoped that the schematic map printed in the inside back cover may help our comprehension. It reminds us there were two exiles recorded in The Tanach, the first to Assyria and the second to Babylon. Our schematic shows that, associated with each national disaster, there were a number of key prophets. In the case of the second, Babylonian, exile there were prophets preceding the disaster, warning of impending doom, those who lived through it as contemporaries and those who came after the trauma, helping to clear up the mess:

> *Readers may want at this point to refer to the schematic map*
> *printed in the back inside cover. It reminds us, in basic terms,*
> *of those two traumatic exiles from the lands of Israel.*

Both exiles in Bible times were hugely traumatic for the nation of Israel, albeit the country was by then a divided nation, not under one ruler. The second exile was the more traumatic, however, as it had been preceded 135 years earlier by the Assyrian invasion from which southern Judah should have learned the necessary spiritual lesson. Far from it, Judah was arguably even more rebellious than northern Israel had been. The three prophets who hold our attention right now are Daniel, Zechariah and Ezekiel. Each was a contemporary of the exile and directly impacted at a personal level. Whilst they prophesied to their own generation, both Jews and non-Jews have long held that their prophecies have both a near-term and a long-term future implication and resonance. Accordingly they remain deeply interesting to us, today. These prophecies have an eschatological echo which we shall explore in the next chapter.

At the end . . .

Scripture teaches that at the end of the present era Messiah Jesus will return in personal, bodily form (Acts 1:11). We do not know precisely when this will occur. Accordingly, some people will be taken by surprise and so will be caught out, like the man who fails to anticipate that his own house will be burgled (Luke 12: 39-40). Jesus taught about *end-time* events in some detail in Matthew chapters 24 and 25, and the consequent need for believers to be alert, faithful and involved in practical witnessing.

In the broad area of eschatology there are a number of themes. We have just referred to Messiah's second coming, but associated with this are the realities of resurrection of the dead and of judgment. Heaven and Hell represent the final states. There will be a time of the rule of Christ in this world, a period often called The Millennium. Prior to Messiah's return there will be a period of unprecedented trouble (often called The Great Tribulation) when Christians and Jews should anticipate active persecution reminiscent of persecutions of the past, yet on a more widespread, global, scale. There is debate and sometimes controversy about the precise details, timing and ordering of all this. Sometimes this controversy causes friction – and even outright schism – between Christians who really ought to know better! Your author simply accepts the view set out by J.E. Church (Joe Church) in his 1933 book "Every Man A Bible Student"[6] where he sets out some of the broad themes revealed in Scripture but counsels against dogmatism, as we simply do not know the full ins- and outs- of all this! The prophet Daniel was told that the whole meaning of what had been revealed to him as a prophet would be "sealed" away until the End Time (Daniel 8:26). This implies that towards the end of the present age there will be an *unsealing* of prophecy, so we should expect that, at the right time, there will be broad consensus amongst believing Christians on what is happening in the world. As always, our legitimate question remains today, as in every generation past, "how close are we to the end?" Each past generation has sought reverently to weigh these things, but there has been added impetus since the recreation of the State of Israel in 1948.

Why did Jesus give us clear teaching and warning? Why is there so much in Scripture on the Last Days and the End Time? The answer, surely, is that properly understood and applied, eschatology has a powerful positive significance for believers in the here and now! It is to be a source of comfort (1 Thessalonians 4: 18), of encouragement (1 Corinthians 15: 58), of challenge to watchfulness and faithful service, and the assurance of reward (Matthew 25: 14-30). Because our time is limited, Believers are to use faithfully the witnessing opportunities that are ours. Because of the certainty of our Lord's return, we are to be filled with hope and courage.

The Day of the Lord

This is a term used by Old Testament prophets, as early as Amos in the eighth century BC, to tell of a time when God will intervene in history, principally for

---

6 A revised, updated and expanded version of Joe Church's book is now available under the CPI imprint and titled "The Bible Student". His updated and expanded study on "The Second Coming" is incorporated as Chapter 7 to *this* book. The updated Joe Church book is freely available as individual PDF studies for download from the CPI website. It continues to be a valuable resource.

the purpose of judgment. So "the day of the Lord" is also called the day of the Lord's anger in Zephaniah 2:2 (KJV). Use of this term in the Old Testament is not one hundred per cent consistent, but generally it speaks of that future judgment, such as in Joel 3:14-21 and Malachi 4:5. Sometimes prophecy of a near-term event is merged with the future end time, the immediate judgment being a preview (or 'type') of the still to come end-time Day of the Lord. Isaiah 13:5-10, and Joel 1:15 - 2:11 are examples. When used in the New Testament, 'Day of the Lord' always means the end time.

The final *Day* of the Lord is characterised as a day of judgment, darkness and gloom with a darkening of the sun, moon and stars (Isaiah 13-10; Joel 2:31; Matthew 24:29; Revelation 6:12). Nations will be judged for their rebellion against God's people and King. Israel is told not to be eager for that Day as she also will suffer judgment (Amos 5:18-20). Yet a "remnant" will be saved by looking toward the Messiah they once rejected (Joel 2:32; Zechariah 12:10). Many Christians see present day events leading towards this scenario.

In the New Testament the corollary terms *day of our Messiah Jesus* (1 Corinthians 1:8), *day of the Lord Jesus* (1 Corinthians 5:5 ; and 2 Corinthians 1:14) and *day of Messiah* (Philippians 1-10 and 2-16) are more personal and positive, pointing towards final events related to true Believers who will escape the wrath of God (1 Thessalonians 5:9). When that day comes, the earth will be renewed and purified through fire (2 Peter 3:10-13). In Revelation the final purging seems to come *after* the 1,000-year reign of Messiah Jesus (Revelation 21:1).

At this point we should note in general terms the diversity of understandings (opinions) of these events under the general heading of eschatology. *Our* focus in this must be on the views of those who hold the Bible to be the 'ultimate source of appeal' in matters of faith and doctrine, and we prudently avoid the ever-fluid 'beliefs' of those church people of a 'liberal' (i.e. non- Bible- believing) persuasion. They appear to have little of value to add, in terms of understanding; rather the opposite, they can be a source of confusion.

Yet even evangelical scholars differ in their understandings about the beginning point of "the Day of the Lord" in relation to other events that are prophesied in Scripture. Three evangelical views have a degree of prevalence in this twenty-first century. They suggest variously that the day of the Lord will commence: (**1**) at the beginning of the seven year period *prior* to Messiah Jesus coming to earth, when a "man of lawlessness" will be revealed and make a covenant with Israel (2 Thessalonians 2:3 and cf Daniel 9:27); or (**2**) following an "abomination of desolation" in which the "man of lawlessness" will pose as God (Matthew 24:15 KJV; 2 Thessalonians 2:4) at the middle of this seven year period; or (**3**) later in the seven year period at the outpouring of God's wrath

(Revelation 16: 1). There are associated differences of opinion about whether or not "the church" is present or absent during these crucial events.

Finally, as regards the future Day of the Lord as prophesied in Scripture, we should note four associated themes that recur. These are somewhat mysterious to Christians and possibly speak both literally and metaphorically (at the same time?). We need to hold these themes in tension with each other as we try to decipher the future: (**1**) biblical passages citing phenomenal celestial signs of that Day (Isaiah 13:10; Joel 2:31 and 3:15; Matthew 24:29; Revelation 6:12); (**2**) the sequence of judgments that focus on seals, trumpets and bowls in the book of Revelation; (**3**) the interrelation of the wrath revealed in Revelation 6:16 to a series of "seal" judgments; and (**4**) the appearance of *the man of lawlessness* in 2 Thessalonians 2:3. On account of these complexities some Christians are prone to argue bitterly. Surely they are foolish in this. Whilst sufficient has been revealed that we need to know from Scripture, yet we presently must perceive these things *as through a glass darkly* (1 Corinthians 13:12, to borrow a phrase from the apostle Paul, somewhat out of its correct context!). In other words it is not easy to understand and it is not meant to be. Your author is certain, as a commentator on all this, that at the right time (still in the future) many of these things will become abundantly plain to true Believers. But not, of course, to unbelievers . . .

CHAPTER 4

ISRAEL'S CENTRAL ROLE

Israel is my firstborn son (Exodus 4:22).

Fourteen one-thousandths

Bear this statistic in mind as you read through this chapter and consider the relentless aggressive focus on Israel by the United Nations and the western media. The world's total land mass is 148,940,000 Km2. Israel's land mass is 22,145 Km2 *which is fourteen one-thousandths of one per cent of the planet's total land mass.* Yet it is within this tiny sliver of planet Earth that *the world at large* is determined to deny to the Israeli people, except on terms that might well be regarded as rendering it a physically un-defendable country, a place of guaranteed safety. But perhaps that is the real point? The world does not want the Jewish people to have a place of safety and security. In reflecting on this we must bear in mind God's promises to a *defined* People group of a *particular* parcel of land . . .

In 2021 the United Nations General assembly passed 14 resolutions singling out the Jewish state. It is notable that out of twenty resolutions specifically criticising a nation, seventy percent focus on Israel. The political driver behind these efforts is the delegitimization and 'demonization' of Israel. One UN resolution (# A/76/L.14) places the blame solely on Israel for the lack of peace in the Middle East yet makes no mention of terror attacks and human rights violations by the Palestinian Authority, Hamas or the PIJ (Palestinian Islamic Jihad). The European Union (and sadly Britain, which in its Foreign Office organisation has a long history of anti-Semitism and anti-Israelism) broadly backed these resolutions, but signally failed to introduce a single resolution on human rights abuses in China, Venezuela, Saudi Arabia, Cuba, Turkey, Pakistan, Vietnam, Algeria or a host of other countries. Since 2015 the UN General Assembly has passed 115 resolutions condemning Israel and only 45 against other countries.

Why is the world's ire, hatred and relentless partisan scrutiny so focused on an area of *fourteen one-thousandths of one percent* of the world's surface? Is the real reason spiritual in nature? If so, precisely which spirits are in evidence? Surely Australian writer Kelvin Crombie hits the proverbial nail right on the head when he writes "perhaps the world system just does not want to see that there is a God, as a restored and harmonious Church would be the clearest evidence to the existence of God; or of the God who has a covenant relationship with the nation of Israel"[1].

Whither Israel?

This is a relatively short chapter, not because our subject is unimportant, but because the question of Israel has been comprehensively addressed by so many other able writers, in more detail, and with perhaps more authority than your author hopes to achieve here[2]. In this chapter we want only to make a few salient points, especially for those readers who may not, hitherto, have considered Israel in the *last days*, or indeed in the *end-time*, scenarios.

We suggest that *the end time* cannot be properly understood in the absence of a clear biblical insight into God's ongoing purposes for His people, Israel. Nor, indeed, can we decipher current events without a clear Israel perspective. Your author strongly recommends that people should not attempt to 'read' every news bulletin and global development solely from the Israel perspective. Such an approach is, we believe, adopted by some of what might fairly be described as *on the 'fringes'* of biblical interpretation. These interpreters have the right general idea, but are apt to interpret the world through a very narrow prophetic lens and draw predictable (and sometimes repetitive) interpretations that may in themselves be questionable; even highly questionable, on occasions. We repeat, however, that a clear Biblical insight into God's persisting activity in, and around, Israel is extraordinarily helpful in these, our present times.

There are essentially three predominant perspectives on the question of Israel. The first is **the World's view**. In speaking in this way we are styling 'the World' as all that mass of Mankind at present ill-disposed towards its Creator God and resistant to His ultimate purpose expressed through Yeshua His Son – our Messiah. The World's view of Israel is that it is both a nuisance and an aberration. Israel is seen as a danger to 'peace' as a supposedly non-legitimate State, foisted upon the world-community through Europe's collective guilt at

---

1 "Israel, Jesus and Covenant", Kelvin Crombie, Heritage Resources Pty Ltd, 2017, page 389
2 See further reading section at the back of this book for some worthwhile suggestions to
   address this question.

Europe's unleashing of the Shoah/Holocaust in the 1940s. The World's view today is essentially hostile to Israel at a political level, and hostile to Jewish people, at a practical level. This view, whilst claiming to be anti-Israel (or 'anti-Zionist'), is normatively anti-Semitic and often does not try to disguise the fact. **The World** will try to 'solve' its Israel problem in its own way and in the light of its own 'wisdom'. For the past 40 years the World has sought a "final settlement" or even a "final solution" to this 'question'. The preferred mechanism has been something called a "two-state solution", but this is presently being amended to a "one-state solution". Yet the outcome for Israeli Jews seems to be much the same . . .

The favoured "solution" to the World's Israel-problem seems to be to corral the Israeli people (and in this they mean Jews, as many Israelis are actually of Arab extraction and live safely and contentedly within Eretz Israel's national borders) into small, solely Jewish-governed areas. These anticipated Jewish areas will not be contiguous, nor defensible in any realistic understanding of that term 'defensible'. We wonder whether the term 'Jewish ghetto' may most aptly describe the World's ambition for Israel's collective security within its own land. A useful proxy for 'the World' in this context might be considered to be The United Nations Organisation (UN) which has been singularly anti-Israel almost since the UN's inception in 1945, even before the rebirth of Israel in 1948. Today the UN acts as both judge and jury in its condemnation of Israel, having issued more 'resolutions' about Israel than about any other country on the planet!

At the time of preparing this book, a "one-state solution" had recently been aired, in the context that several Arab nations had settled upon a form of peace with Israel ('The Abraham Accords') which, in turn, had reduced the so-called *Palestinian question* to one of secondary status. At the same time Syria was in civil war and Egypt was deeply concerned about terrorist violence within its society. At a practical level, some of the support for a two-state solution had simply evaporated. A one-state solution seemed to entail the political cantonment of Israel and an enhancement of the political rights of Arab Israelis (as opposed, presumably, to Jewish Israelis) as a form of *positive discrimination*. Demographically, the Arab population seems likely to overtake the Jewish population[3], so a one-state solution may prove to be a quicker mechanism to undermine the reality of Israel as a Jewish state, than the stalled 'two-state solution'.

The second predominant worldview on Israel emerges from within those institutions that collectively are referred to as **"the Church"**. In using this term

---

3 Note that population data seems to be as confused and debated as any other question about Israel and 'the Palestinians'. Received wisdom, however, is that eventually the Arab Israeli population will overtake the Jewish Israeli population *at some point*. At precisely what point is open to debate as this question is highly politicised!

your authors draw a clear distinction between "the church" as a series of Man-made institutions, versus the *spiritual* Body of Messiah Jesus collectively referred to as "church" in the sense of being His *corporate body*, of which Messiah Jesus is the Head. We would style that Christ-focused "church" as being *the true church*, and Jesus Himself surely made that distinction (Matthew 16: 18).

The institutional Church's collective understanding of Israel, both as a political / geographical entity, as well as a cultural people collectively and globally thought of as "Israel", can be summarised by the term **Replacement Theology** (or "Fulfillment Theology" which, at a practical level, amounts to the same thing). Via this 'theology', the institutional church perceives itself as being *the new Israel*, having assumed responsibility from, and replaced, 'old Israel' which it sees as being terminated by, in, and through "the New Covenant"[4].

'Replacement Theology' is sometimes modified into 'Two Covenant Theology' in the minds of some church folk[5] who may be slightly better disposed towards Israel. The idea here is that Jewish people do not need to hear the good news of Yeshua Messiah as they will be 'saved' (if at all) by adherence to Rabbinic Judaism and their observance of the Torah. By this view Christians are to be 'saved' through their altogether easier and more comfortable "New Covenant" of grace, wherein Jesus has already "paid the price" for the penitent sinner. Jews, by contrast, have to 'earn' their Salvation through Torah observance. We surely do not need to state that this obtuse view is nowhere supported in Scripture, nor the specific teachings of Jesus.

The third popular view on Israel can best be summarised by the term **Classical Zionism**[6] which understands that His covenants with Israel are not abrogated by God, nor are they 'replaced' by the New Covenant. This view, rather, sees the New Covenant as augmenting the older covenants and being the end-point in God's covenantal purposes. Classical Zionism is the broad view of the author of *this* book. Classical Zionism takes the text of the Bible in its plainest sense and accordingly sees God's unconditional prophetic promises to Israel as remaining in force and not 'fulfilled' in, or via, some other entity. **Enlargement Theology** is the prism through which we understand God's over-arching purposes, as opposed to Replacement Theology. Rev Alex Jacob's seminal work "The Case for Enlargement Theology" [7] is the clearest exposition of this hermeneutical approach.

---

4 This idea emerged in the Byzantine era and was inherited by Catholicism, Orthodoxy and (some) Protestants. In its earlier Catholic manifestation, this "Replacement" worldview became a considerable political and social reality in the Dark Ages. It has permeated the institutional churches ever since.

5 Often of a more 'liberal' persuasion.

6 e.g. as defined in David Pawson's book "Defending Christian Zionism"

7 See further reading section at the back of this book

All of this has been widely explored in the literature before. Liberal Christians[8] do not see the Bible as authoritative. Thus, in their own estimation, they possess their 'get out of gaol free card', and can ignore Israel as an issue. They "interpret" the Bible using their hermeneutic of eisegesis (reading-in to Scripture what they want or expect to be there) and use that mechanism to eliminate Israel from God's eternal story.

God's dealings with Israel

In my 2009 book "Rebel Church", I made the simple observation that Christians who fail to gain a thoroughly biblical insight into God's ongoing purposes for Israel will be increasingly perplexed in the years ahead. Why? As Israel continually pops up in the world's media and some Church folk state, categorically and with certainty, that Israel has a distinct and continuing role in God's end-time purposes, so naive or biblically illiterate Christians will be torn between the World's unswervingly anti-Israel (and pro Palestinian) narrative, whilst the Bible seems prima facie to demonstrate God's equally unswerving commitment to, and ongoing purposes for, His ancient Covenant People[9]. What to believe? Whom to believe? Something has to give! In this situation it is generally Biblical exegesis that "gives" and many church folk find it impossible to swim against the tide of anti-Israel rhetoric.

The week this chapter was first prepared (mid-May 2021) Israel was again in the media spotlight as a fresh mini 'intifada' was underway. Anti-Semitic sentiment throughout Europe (and indeed under a seemingly pro-Palestinian/anti-Israel President Biden in the USA) was at a post-World War Two all-time high. Biblically astute Christians assess all this anti-Israel hatred in the light of what the Bible reveals of an impending false peace and a false peacemaker associated with Israel's future. Of course some commentators argue that prophecy concerning Israel has all been fulfilled in the past and therefore has no modern relevance. That a Liberal Christian might argue this case is unsurprising, since they do not hold a high view of Scripture and do not base their worldview upon Scripture. When those Christians that are generally biblically astute, Bible-believing and hold a high view of Scripture, argue much the same ('it's all in the past'), we should be rather more surprised. Why? Because many key prophecies concerning Israel have never been fulfilled, as this table reminds us:

---

8 Those holding a low view of Scripture
9 We should add that there is widespread lack of understanding amongst church-attending Christians about the nature of the interrelationship of what some call "the old covenant" versus what is generally thought of as "the new covenant".

GOD'S DEALINGS WITH ISRAEL / THE HEBREW PEOPLE	BIBLE	SUMMARY COMMENTS AND KEY QUESTIONS
God's promise of an heir to Abram is immediately followed by the promise of land. This is God's covenant with Abram.	Gen 15: 7 & 18	Here God promises to Abram's descendants a specific land – bounded by the river of Egypt to the Euphrates; the existing 10 small tribes in possession are named. Sweep of land from Iraq to Egypt (?).
Abram becomes Abraham – the father of many nations	Gen 17: 4	God promises to be the father of Abraham's descendants – for males the sign of circumcision is required. For the Church, circumcision no longer required – see Galatians 5: 2.
Through Abraham's offspring all nations will be blessed	Gen 22: 18	Generally understood to be via Jesus the Messiah and through His true Church – the body of Christ
The Edomites were cursed because they rejoiced at the desolation of the 'inheritance' of Israel	Ezek 35: 15	Plainly the inheritance of Israel that was 'desolate' was the lands of Israel. Those who rejoice in Israel's woes seem to be paid back in kind. Is this still true today?
Prophecies against Israel's neighbours	Ezek chapters 25 thru 30	Israel has always been under attack (why?). Is there a read-across to the woes of the modern enemies (neighbours) of Israel?
Exile followed by home-coming	Ezek 36: 8 & 37:14	Prophecies often have a near term and a long term outworking. (Two audiences – the one for whom the prophecy was originally written, and for us – succeeding generations). There were 2 major exiles in OT times – to Assyria and to Babylonia. After a period of punishment the Israelites were allowed by God to return home.

Israel's geography	Ezek 47: 15 thru 23	This is a more granular description of Israel's inheritance.
The Psalmist remembers God's gift of the Holy Lands to Israel	Ps 78: 54	God brought the Israelites to their lands as an inheritance. He drove other tribes out before them. Did God have a "right" to do this?
God revealed His laws to Israel	Ps 147: 19	He has done so for no other nation – they do not know His laws.
I will put Israel in her own land, never more to be uprooted	Amos 9: 15	When was this prophecy fulfilled? If it hasn't been fulfilled, when will it be? See also Jeremiah 16: 14-15.
Moses is Israel's accuser – says Jesus	John 5: 45	God continued to work out His purposes in the Lord Jesus' time. The Lord Jesus recognised this.
The terms on which Israel may live there	Jer 7: 5	If you change your ways, deal justly, protect aliens, then I will let you live there forever and ever. What does forever and ever mean? Why the emphasis? Is this the same 'forever and ever' as in Galatians 1:5?
Loss of lands because of sin	Dan 9: 4 ff	As throughout the OT, Israel's punishment is directly associated with her sin (e.g. verse 11). This is a consistent message throughout the OT.
Israel is the apple of God's eye	Zech 2: 8	What happens to those who still attack the apple of God's eye – is this true today?
Can a Nation be born in a day?	Isa 66: 8	Some see this as a prophetic insight into 14 May 1948. Are they wrong to do so?

Jerusalem will be "an immovable rock for all Nations"	Zech 12: 3	When in the past did this happen? What is the meaning of this prophecy if it yet lies in the future? Are we beginning to see this becoming true in our own day?
All nations will rise up against Israel	Zech 14: 2 - 4	Has this prophecy been fulfilled (especially verse 4)? If not when will it be?
God's help to Israel – Israel survives!	Ps 124	But surely this is still true?
God remembers His covenant – and will establish an everlasting covenant	Ezek 16: 60	But surely this is still true?
God's promise of peace to Israel	2 Sam 7: 10	No longer disturbed . . . has this yet been fulfilled?
	Heb 3: 18 – 4: 1	The Jews were unable to 'enter' because of their unbelief – but will there come a time when they do believe and may therefore 'enter their rest'?
God's plans remain forever	Ps 33: 10 - 11	The Lord thwarts the plans of men (and nations) but His plans stand forever. Can we apply this to the Jews and to Israel?
Deliverance promised	Micah 2: 12 - 13	Is there a near term as well as far term outworking of this?
God promises to bring Israel back	Lev 26: 42 - 45	Is there a near term as well as far term outworking of this? In the light of other evidence, this underlines the all-time aspect of Israel's connection with the lands.

New covenant foretold	Jer 31: 31 - 34	When will this happen, if it has not *already* happened?! Note with which Nation this new covenant is "cut".
God will bear his holy arm before all nations	Isaiah 52: 10	This cannot refer to Cyrus because Israel was redeemed from just one nation – not all nations. So when will this happen? Where does 1948 fit into this?
Future unprecedented peace for Israel?	Isaiah 63: 7	Jer 31:28, 31: 36, 32: 42, 32: 37 – 41, 33: 6 – 8. When did this happen if not in future? Also, Isaiah 19: 23-25.

Notes:

A recurrent theme through the OT is God's husband-like love for His people Israel, and their continual rebellion against Him. The promise of a *new covenant* is explicit, but this does not negate the older covenant(s). Rather, it enlarges the older covenants. If God's covenant (contract) with Israel is said to be inherited by others (i.e. the Church) because of its repudiation by Israel, then surely God would have said this explicitly in the NT. If any modern contract was to be assigned from one party to another, a lawyer would express this explicitly – is God less diligent than a modern lawyer?!

The Bible verses tabled above, although random and arguably not set clearly in any context, nevertheless appear to support the view that God's promises are made and kept for all time. The very fact of Israel's survival (or rather, the Jewish people's survival) through 4 millennia of attack suggests that God is indeed true to His promise, *unless you take the view that some other spiritual power has been protecting Israel.*

Why should we believe that Rome's enforced exile of the Israelites (actually the Second-Century Judeans and Galileans) would have an outcome different from that already experienced by Israel after the Assyrian and the Babylonian experiences of exile? The Roman exile was longer and infinitely more painful, because the sin was the greatest of all (rejection of the Messiah). But in the same way we expect the return of the Messiah at the final crisis in world history, should we not also expect a return of the Hebrew people to their inheritance? And should we not expect that those who oppose this claiming of inheritance (i.e. actively oppose modern Israel's right to exist) to be themselves opposed by God, and to suffer the same sort of consequences suffered by Israel's ancient enemies?

God's unhesitating love for Israel is expressed beautifully in Jeremiah chapter 31 and leads straight into the prophecy of a new covenant (Jer 31: 31) understood to be a covenant through the Lord Jesus and with all people – the old Abrahamic and Mosaic covenants are enlarged by the new.

If God's "forever" promises to the Jews can be broken by God, then can we have confidence in His NT "forever" promises?

The Jews have certain obligations to 'aliens' in their midst, but by implication those aliens also have obligations to their hosts [e.g. Romans 13:1 and Jeremiah 29:7]. This may go some way to explain the present intractable issues between Israel and the 'Palestinians.' In this regard it should be noted that the use of the name 'Palaestina' (or in full *Syria Palaestina*) by the Romans at the close of the Bar Kokhba revolt (ended AD 136) was part of Roman policy of extinguishing the memory of Jews from their lands (what today we would call ethnic cleansing). 'Palaestina' was derived from ancient *Philistia* – the most intractable of Israel's ancient enemies – the Philistines. Classical scholars have used the name 'Palestine' ever since to describe the biblical lands, but note that 'Palestine' was not a political reality until 1919 when the British used it as a title for the lands ceded to British control by the League of Nations. It is an interesting fact that the name chosen, although scholarly, has certain theological - even spiritual - overtones.

If the OT promises and NT confirmations are taken at face value, then the widespread attempts to undermine modern Israel may also have theological and spiritual overtones.

Covenant theology: the promises of the covenant undergo expansion (via the Church) but they never suffer abrogation. The NT does not *emphasise* a literal restoration of Israel. Why? Partly because the final out-workings of the Jewish War ending in AD70 and the Bar Kochba revolt of AD 132-136 had not yet happened at the time the New Testament was written. So the question had not arisen (?). In any case, the Gentile church began to see itself as being the future of 'Israel'. But an argument from silence – i.e. the NT does emphasise the literal restoration – cannot be conclusive, especially when set against the other clear pointers that the Bible gives us, starting with the old Moses covenant. * see David Pawson "*Israel in the New Testament*". Whilst the NT does not emphasise the literal restoration, it certainly alludes to it in many places, and David Pawson's book is an excellent resource to pursue an in-depth exploration of God's purposes in this regard.

Being honest

In reviewing the above Table and associated Notes, readers are encouraged to ask themselves – and indeed, *to try to answer for themselves* – the general questions that it raises. The prophecies are sufficiently direct and unequivocal for us to 'pose' the questions in the way we have, above. God has given us clarity in His intentions, so we are entitled to ask in each specific prophetic revelation, * has this happened (and if so when)? * if this has not happened are we right to assume that its fulfillment lies in the future (and if not, why not?). And finally, * how does this foretelling speak to us today? These are of course vitally important questions. It is ultimately dishonest to try to 'dodge' or ignore them, as these questions will simply not go away.

As we draw this chapter towards its conclusion, let us summarise. So many excellent Christian writers have explored this subject over so many years, both before - and especially since - the recreation of the State of Israel in 1948, that we can be sure that the broad outline and much of the detail of God's ongoing purposes is well enough understood today – at least by those prepared to engage spiritually and biblically with God's revealed purposes. The Bible is clear! If we are unclear it may just be that we do not want to engage honestly with the Bible!

The reason why so much of 'the church' is all at 'sixes and sevens' about this matter is because 'the church' is uncomfortable with the implications and conclusions that must be drawn. Much of the institutional church remains in denial about Israel, and too many church folk are, in any case, woefully disconnected from Scripture. That Israel will be a huge stumbling block to the institutional churches in the closing stages of this age, and by the same token to many individual Christians, is something that your author explored in the book "Rebel Church". It is hugely ironic that much of the institutional church seems readier to speak and engage with Rabbinic Judaism[10], in various interfaith forums, than with Messianic Judaism – that is with those Jewish people who <u>do</u> follow Yeshua ha Massiasch – Jesus the Messiah. It is almost as though Messianic Jews constitute, for the institutional churches, an embarrassing and inconvenient *elephant in the room*, and to engage with our *professing* and *declared* Jewish brothers and sisters raises too many uncomfortable questions.

---

10 which remains ill disposed towards the reality of Yeshua

Overjoyed

Not so, however, for many individual Christians who do search the Scriptures, in true Berean style. Many, many individual Christians are indeed excited and overjoyed at what God continues to do amongst His chosen peoples, and at the very evident outworking of His prophetically declared purposes.

We will conclude with one obvious and (we would argue) undeniable truth. In the book of Zechariah, written during the Babylonian captivity and anticipating a future return to Israel, God gives to His prophet a vision of the future which, in all likelihood, Zechariah himself did not fully understand. Chapters 12 to 14 of Zechariah look far into the future, beyond Israel's contemporary problems in exile, to a certain "day". In these chapters the phrase "on that day" is used some fifteen times, and points towards a future marked by the security of God's People, as a People finally and definitively cleansed by the Lord. Whilst some people of the Replacement/Fulfillment hermeneutic may consider that this is all somehow fulfilled in and through "the church", this is a view that is hard to sustain when confronted with the specific terms of the prophecy itself.

As we have already asked in our Table above, in Zechariah chapter 12 verse 2 God declares "**Look! I will make Jerusalem a cup that causes staggering for the peoples who surround the city**". Today we might ask, precisely who surrounds Jerusalem? Is it "just" the Jordanians, Syrians and Egyptians? Or is it the entire World that surrounds Jerusalem, figuratively in the shape of its United Nations Organisation? The World has decided that Jerusalem as a city must be divided, with half "allowed" to Israel and half given to "the Palestinians". Whether this will happen in practice remains to be seen, but to divide this city is very much the World's agenda. No alternative possibility is today entertained – in particular that Eretz Israel should have the ancient city as its recognised capital.

In Zechariah 13 verse 3 God declares that *on that day* He will "**make Jerusalem a heavy stone for all the peoples. All who try to lift it will injure themselves severely when the nations of the world gather against her**". The dividing of Jerusalem may have been allowed by God during Israel's near 1900 year exile from her lands, but it seems that God has decreed that Jerusalem must be reserved for his Chosen People when they return.

And therein lies the rub! They *have* returned, and the time of the Gentiles has run its course (as Jesus said it would[11] – see Luke 21:24 (also Romans

---

[11] In Luke 21:24, Jesus speaks of future events including the destruction of Jerusalem and His return. He says that "Jerusalem will be trampled underfoot by the Gentiles, until the times of the Gentiles are fulfilled" (ESV). A similar phrase is found in Romans 11:25, where the Apostle Paul says, "A partial hardening has come upon Israel, until the fullness of the Gentiles has come in" (ESV). See David Pawson, "Israel in the New Testament" for a full exploration of this subject.

11:25)). Yet the World has declared its opposition to Eretz Israel – directly – and therefore to God's purposes for Jerusalem. We must come back to that term "the World" as we defined it above – all that mass of Mankind ill-disposed to its Creator God and living in opposition to His purposes. It is not only the political machinery of the World that opposes Israel, it is also popularly that mass of Mankind. Every attempt to impose a 'peace' upon Israel has foundered, and those politicians and pundits who seek to impose such a 'peace' seem to be unseated relatively quickly. Elsewhere God has declared "**those who bless you I will bless; those who curse you I will curse**" (Genesis 12:3). In this God was speaking directly to Abraham, but God's promise has long been understood to reflect His eternal purposes for Israel. Can today's multiple and multiplying global woes and uncertainties be explained, at least in part, by the World's attempt to curse Israel?

Zechariah chapter 14 tells us that the world will rise up against Jerusalem. Whilst some Bible commentators tell us that the fulfillment of this prophecy lies in the past, there are two powerful objections to this idea: (1) when read in the context of the entire prophecy across chapters 12 to 14, it is clear this lies yet in the future as part of the End time scenario. And (2) the world collectively has never in history *combined* to 'rise up' against Jerusalem. Taken literally then, this must lie still in the future. Today we can indeed see a time on our political horizons when, through the institution that Men call their "United Nations", the World will indeed 'rise up' in the way prophesied by Zechariah, whether politically, militarily, or both.

Finally we turn to the prophet Joel, who also prophesied in the context of the Babylonian captivity of Israel. Whilst his message is directly to the people in exile, indirectly it is for us, as again we must comment that it has not yet been fulfilled in its entirety: "**For behold, in those days and at that time, when I restore the fortunes of Judah and Jerusalem, I will gather all the nations and bring them down to the Valley of Jehoshaphat. And I will enter into judgment with them there, on behalf of my people and my heritage Israel, because they have scattered them among the nations and have divided up my land**" (Joel 3:1-2). Many Christians understand this as also referencing a restored Israel that will be opposed by "all the nations". God will ultimately bring these opposing nations to judgment.

Israel will have a central role in *the end time*. Arguably, Israel has held a central role in *The Last Days* as well, as we have previously defined that term. During 'the church era', the institutional churches have themselves never been far removed from outright persecution of Jews[12]. And whilst Israel rejects her

---

12 See "Father Forgive Us – A Christian Response to the Church's Heritage of Jewish Persecution" by Fred Wright 2002, Monarch Press

Messiah, so in consequence the world at large has its time of blessing in being able to receive Israel's Messiah whilst God's Covenant is enlarged to encompass all Mankind (see Romans 11; 13, 15, 25(b), and 31). Gentiles are able to respond to God's call only because Israel has rejected her Messiah. But this window of opportunity for Gentiles must eventually close, as Israel shall be again – finally and collectively – brought into the blessings of the New Covenant era.

Praise God indeed! In the words of the apostle Paul as he contemplated these profound mysteries, "**Oh, the depths of the riches and the wisdom and the knowledge of God! How unsearchable his judgments, and untraceable his ways!**" (Romans 11: 33).

CHAPTER 5

MAPPING THE END TIMES

keep reminding God's people of these things.
Warn them before God against quarrelling about words. It is of no value,
and only ruins those who listen (2 Timothy 2:14).

A clear roadmap?

It would be wonderful, would it not, to have a clear 'roadmap' that sets out with precision how the world will end and how God will finally work out His eternal purposes. Such a roadmap is one thing that God has definitely declined to give us. Even had He done so, the World at large would have rejected it as being mere make-believe, in precisely the same way the World has, by and large, rejected every other element of God's Self- revelation. The last days are, in any case, characterised by "scoffing" (2 Peter 3: 3).

Some Christians do indeed provide what they see as a definitive road-map to 'plot' the end times. Most notably these scenarios are mapped out within that strain of biblical interpretation known as "Dispensationalism" (see chapter 2 of this book). The efforts of Dispensationalists are well meaning and take Biblical prophecy extremely seriously. On that basis they are to be commended. Indeed, in some outlines their broad conclusions have a certain degree of merit – in other words some of their scenarios are likely to be correctly defined. The 'trouble' with their outlines, however, is that they tend to introduce certain concepts and terminology that are extra-biblical, and often they hold to these (man-made?) theories with a tenacity bordering on the obsessional. In turn, some are wont to break fellowship with other believers who do not hold to their theologies[1].

---

1 The valid point is sometimes made that the Bible is not a systematic theology. God has determinedly not given to mankind a systematic theology in His Word. Rather He has given us the means to Salvation and to relationship with Him. In short, the entire Bible is about Jesus, and God's eternal purpose is wrapped-up in Jesus. This is not to suggest that we cannot be 'systematic' in our appreciation of God's purposes, nor see many truths systematically applied by God. Nor is it to suggest that God's Self-revelation is in any way haphazard – the claim of those who are 'universalists' and believe that all religions somehow lead to God. But it is to suggest that 'theologies' can all too often represent Men's desire to impose upon God's revelation their own agendas – and sometimes these agendas depart markedly from God's purposes.

In the 1930s a missionary in Rwanda, Joe Church, wrote "Every Man a Bible Student", which set out certain key recurring biblical themes. Joe Church would follow these themes from the Old Testament into the New. His book was well received and ran to multiple printings over the next 30 years. It was re-issued by *Christian Publications International* in 2012 as a completely revised and re-written book ("The Bible Student")[2] as it remains such a very useful resource in the library of any Christian. Joe Church, who was a Dispensationalist in his overall outlook, provided a study on "The Second Coming" which is the basis of Study # 44 in "The Bible Student" of 2012. We incorporate this Study as Chapter seven to this book. Despite his Dispensational leanings, Joe Church consciously avoided the trap of being overly dogmatic about end-time details. Indeed he wisely cautioned against dogmatism as he acknowledged that some aspects of Christ's second coming remain opaque, even to the dedicated student of Scripture. Joe Church's approach was surely wise and your author concurs with his broad outline set out in our chapter seven.

Can we 'map' with clarity beyond what Joe Church provided? Tentatively, we would say 'yes', we can take this a step further, but should do so without being dogmatic. Jesus graciously provided for us clear clues as to what to expect in the end time. Matthew Chapters 24 and 25 provide this and readers may wish to pause at this point and simply read what the Lord said. Strictly speaking, what Yeshua gave us is everything that we need and on that basis we really ought to be familiar with it. There will be "signs", and we are to be sufficiently awake to 'read' those signs correctly. That is what Yeshua said, so let's make sure we do it!

The biggest question of all for a Disciple of Jesus, and where Scripture seems obscure, is, will there be *two* second comings, one for Christians (sometimes called the 'rapture' – *note a term not found in Scripture*) and then a second one as Jesus returns as Judge? Dispensationalists are not totally agreed on this even amongst themselves,[3] but some believe this to be the case. We must observe, however, that Jesus nowhere speaks about arriving twice in the end-time context, so we think that the idea of a double return is mistaken. Our view (and we think this is borne out by Scripture itself) is that Jesus will return once, and there will be a supernatural gathering of His faithful people at a time of international distress when Mankind as a whole will have rejected all the good that Jesus has achieved and will instead worship a false 'messiah' known variously as the *instead-of Christ* (or 'Antichrist') or 'the Beast'. After

---

2 Presently it is available study by study in PDF format, and can be freely downloaded from the CPI website. See the frontispiece to this book for the CPI website URL.

3 Dispensational theologies, are not uniform or consistent. In this they mirror other purported "systems" of theology.

Jesus returns, He will establish a 1000 year rule[4] on this planet, and Mankind will learn what it means to live under wise and righteous government. At first Mankind will welcome this new form of government, simply because what went before under the Antichrist was so awful. But the old resentments and desire for autonomy (the old Adam and Eve problem) will eventually reassert itself even after Mankind has tasted what good government really is. God releases Satan from the abyss at this point and once again Mankind determines to follow the devil, albeit for a *very* short period. After that God creates a new heaven and a new earth, symbolised in the picture of *the New Jerusalem*.

In outline, this is our understanding and we believe it is consistent with the specifics of Scripture as well as 'making sense' in that Mankind ultimately refuses God's very best even under His righteous and loving direct-rule. Sadly, Mankind is an incorrigible sinner; he demands better government, but refuses it even when perfection in government is demonstrated. If, as we have suggested, the entire period since the return of Messiah Jesus to be at His Father's side has been "the last days" in terms of God's dealings with Mankind, then "the end times" are those times leading up to – and immediately preceding – Christ's return, when definitively, Mankind will have no further excuse for his rebellions. For Mankind, however, "the last days" extends into God's millennial rule on Earth. *Salvation for the individual will still be required during this period*. Messiah's blood shed upon the Cross will still be efficacious (i.e. effective).

Quite why Jesus' rule on earth extends for 1000 years is open to speculation, but speculation is always speculation! We caution against speculation as Mankind will never know *the full answer* until it has been finally revealed in practice. But in *this* book we offer, tentatively and with humility, a possible explanation. All that precedes Messiah's second coming can be summarised - and climaxes - in one word: Armageddon. Given that Armageddon represents Mankind's ultimate folly and ultimate defiance against God and against His People, and given that the results of Armageddon are so devastating, it may well be that it will take the survivors of Mankind some hundreds of years simply to clean up the mess we have created! If so, this clearing up will be done under God's *millennial rule* and by and through God's wisdom. Perhaps eventually Mankind, having emerged from the clean-up task, now lives in a period of total stability under God's rule, but the books of Revelation and Zechariah include the intriguing suggestion that even in this period, there will be a measure of disobedience and reluctance (Revelation 2: 27; Zechariah 14: 16 to 19). How sad! Despite all that Mankind will have seen

---

4 Often referred to as 'the millennial rule' and/or 'the millennium'.

and understood and despite God's righteous direct rule, yet the old seeds of discontent remain in at least some hearts . . .

We readily acknowledge that the above is broadly speculative and can only be considered on that clear basis. We are certainly not dogmatic about this, and nor should our readers be!

Signs – The Moedim

As Mankind approaches the time of Christ's return, so we are to be aware of preceding, and increasingly urgent, signs as already noted. The remainder of *this* chapter sets out a *dashboard of history* which helps us consider the signs of which Yeshua spoke so directly, and to which other parts of the Bible also bear testimony. Any 'dashboard' (or 'control panel') will incorporate instruments with 'readable' outputs that are very often colour-coded as red, amber or green. The point about the approach of Messiah Jesus is that *the warning signs* will move progressively from their historical 'normal' (as green) through into amber and then finally to red. Whilst historically these warning signs can and have 'glowed' amber – or even sometimes red – yet later returned to green, the End Times will be marked by a progressive transition of all signs from amber to red. There will come a time when so many are simultaneously 'glowing' red that *the eyes of faith* will know, with certainty, that we are on the threshold of the Messiah's return.

Down through history every generation has wondered, often with very good reason, whether they were living in the end times. The warnings that Jesus gave have seemed to be coming true – things like widespread war, civil disturbance, the persecution of Believers, disease and moral decay. All have periodically waxed and then waned as issues. In terms of persecution, it seems *unlikely* that the end time will present anything materially worse than what has been seen before except, perhaps, in terms of its global extent/universality and demonic cleverness. Also, perhaps, in the sense that Believers will not be able to move from one place to another to alleviate their suffering, as has sometimes been the case in the past.

On these bases every previous generation in different parts of the world has had reason to ask itself the question, 'is this it?' Peter Sammons recalls his mother saying that when she was still young, at the beginning of World War 2, she wondered whether Adolf Hitler was the Antichrist. Today many would say without hesitation that Hitler was *an* antichrist and endowed with the *spirit* of antichrist, but he was not *the* Antichrist. Dreadful men as political and religious rulers in the past have often had, and been energized by, the spirit of Antichrist, and in effect have been worshipped by their people (think of the

North Korean leader Kim Jong Un today). When populations worship or semi-worship their leader, that leader is always saturated with the spirit of *instead of Christ* ('antichrist').

There has been no time in history when there have not been leaders who expected to be worshipped and/or to be seen as being a deity. Needless to say each has represented a huge threat to those who worship the true God Who Self-identifies as "**the God of Jacob**" (Matthew 22: 32 [5]). Whilst we can undoubtedly be challenged if we seek to map the End Time, your author has previously used the Moedim to 'map' God's salvation purposes prophetically; we looked at this briefly in chapter 3. This is a subject area that demands its own separate and detailed study, but we can at least summarise in simple terms what the Moedim teach collectively about Jesus and God's plan for humanity.

First, what are the Moedim? These are the Hebrew feasts commanded by God and set out in the book of Leviticus, chapter 23. Whilst at first sight these may seem to be very much Old Testament (and Old Covenant) commands, it is undoubtedly true that, prophetically, the seven feasts (Moed = singular, so each feast is a Moed; Moedim = plural, so all seven are collectively *the Moedim*) speak about God's purposes expressed through the life, mission and ministry of the Lord Jesus. The Moedim take their place alongside variously The Tabernacle (Temple), the exodus from Egypt and subsequent entry into the Promised Land, and the life and times of certain Old Testament characters (such as Ruth), and even the Song of Songs, as *each pointing prophetically towards Jesus*. Such pointers are called variously "types" and "shadows". Today a number of Bible teachers are investing increasingly in exploring the various *types* and *shadows* of Messiah Yeshua, found principally in the Old Testament.

So how do the Moedim collectively speak of Jesus, and how does this help us to "map" the last days and the end time? The seven biblical feasts happen on defined days; in the illustrations below they are depicted as 'larger' than they are in reality as six of the seven are day-only events. But the 'pattern' we see below is easy enough to 'lock' into our mind's eye, so we invite readers to try to achieve this for themselves.

Using English names for these festivals, we find they are **Passover** (most Christians are aware of this), **Unleavened Bread** (many who know their Bibles will at least have heard of this), **First Fruits**, **Latter First Fruits** (normatively, Pentecost – again all Christians should be aware of Pentecost), **Trumpets**, **Atonement**, and **Tabernacles**. These *assemblies* map across to certain "Christian" festivals, but the Christian festivals are rather haphazard in reflecting

---

5 See also Exodus 3: 6 and 15; Psalm 20: 1; 46: 7; 81: 1. Used approximately seventeen times. Plus Mark 12: 26; Luke 20: 37; Acts 7: 46.

what are, in reality, profound truths about Yeshua. So, Jesus was raised from the dead on the third day after Passover (First Fruits, not "Easter", and we note that "Easter" is not found in the Bible!). Pentecost falls fifty days after Passover. A modern term to describe *functionally* what Pentecost achieves is 'Latter First Fruits', and interestingly this term originated amongst Messianic Believers.

Yeshua was raised at First Fruits[6] as He is the very first "fruit" of the eternal harvest of those who are raised immortal. The Latter First Fruits period represents the harvesting of all those souls who will follow Yeshua in being "saved" from eternal death. But we are saved on the basis of what Messiah Jesus has achieved at Golgotha, not on any merit of our own.

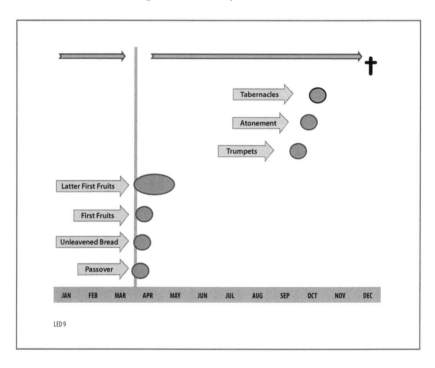

LED 9

The schematic above "maps" the Moedim. The schematic below shows the Christological reality that sits behind each commanded Feast. Three lie in the past, three in our future. And the middle one is happening today! Yeshua was crucified, buried and raised again. That is historical fact and certainty. The Holy Spirit was first poured out at Pentecost (Latter First Fruits) as He is poured out into the lives of all Believers. If Pentecost is considered to be the birthday of the true church (and we think this is a reasonable analogy) then the church age under God's purposes is the age in which we live today. The church age will

---

6 Not at "Easter"!!

only conclude when Yeshua returns. Trumpets, it seems, will herald His return. Some people consider that a reasonable case can be made that the Lord will actually return at Trumpets. It is an interesting possibility . . .

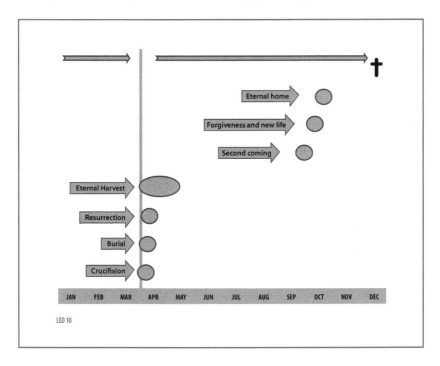

Jesus' purpose in returning (above) is so that forgiveness and new life can be granted eternally, as well as judgment executed on the same basis. Only after these events will Yeshua and His People tabernacle together into eternity. Our schematic below shows that the entire Latter First Fruits period extends from Pentecost until the Lord's return. That much, at least, is non controversial amongst most Christians.

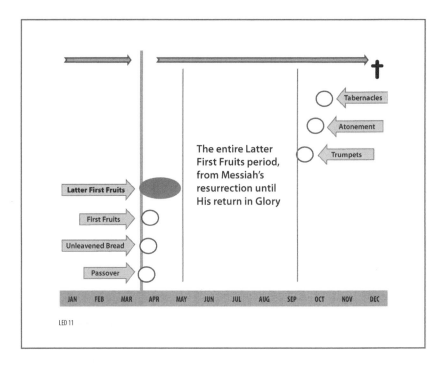

The entire Latter First Fruits period, from Messiah's resurrection until His return in Glory

Tabernacles

Atonement

Trumpets

Latter First Fruits

First Fruits

Unleavened Bread

Passover

JAN FEB MAR APR MAY JUN JUL AUG SEP OCT NOV DEC

LED 11

We can plot these ideas as depicted below, with three events definitely in the past, the fourth happening today and until Jesus returns, and the final three lying as yet in our future. From the viewpoint of this book, with its emphasis on the Last Days, we can add that the World's *Last Days* coincide with what is otherwise thought of as *the church age*. This is God's last offer of safety through the blood of Messiah Jesus. God has styled these as *The Last Days* for a very good reason. They ARE the last days and will cease at the inauguration of the New Heaven and the New Earth (Revelation 21: 22).

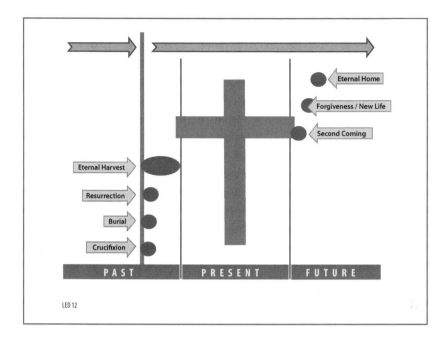

LED 12

In the above schematic, "Present" could in fact be styled as "the Last Days". In terms of what the Moedim collectively mean from the viewpoint of God's eternal purpose, our schematic below adds some further detail. Remember, each Moed is concerned with Jesus:

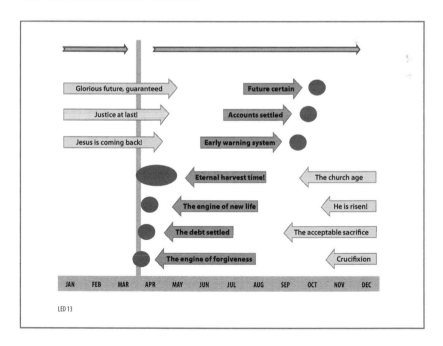

LED 13

Passover, then, is the engine of forgiveness. We can only be forgiven on account of what Jesus has already done for us. Jesus' burial (at Unleavened Bread) is the proof that our debt is settled, because Yeshua is *the* acceptable sacrifice. We should add, God accepts no other sacrifice, only the blood and life of His Own dear Son is acceptable and no other 'sacrifice' is sufficient[7]. Yet He is risen – hallelulia! The engine of new life is His resurrected living body demonstrated on that First Fruits morning – and is eternal life, an incorruptible life, that is shared by all His followers who avail themselves of His blood. Not for nothing are we told that we must be washed in His blood (Revelation 7: 14 specifically, but see also Romans 3:25; Ephesians 1: 7; Colossians 1: 20; Hebrews 10: 19; 1 Peter 1: 18-19; 1 John 1: 7 and Revelation 1: 5).

Harvesting continues until Messiah Jesus returns. He reminds us that *the fields are white to harvest* (John 4: 35) and we are to ask the Lord of the Harvest to *send more workers into the field* (Matthew 9: 38). Surely, these harvesters are needed, their task being a huge one! But Jesus is coming back and Trumpets is God's chosen *early warning* system of this return. Jesus told us of signs to be alert for, and that each sign is to be considered as a shofar blast. Whilst this time of warning will be uncomfortable, yet we are to take comfort that He is on the way. When you hear of these things, says Yeshua, lift up your heads because you KNOW your time of redemption draws near (Luke 21: 28).

The future holds ultimate justice when accounts must be settled. For the impenitent rebel, there will be nowhere to hide, and sadly, no sacrifice left for sin. No wonder we are told THIS is the day of salvation (2 Corinthians 6: 2)[8]. Our glorious eternal future with Yeshua is guaranteed, no ifs, no buts and no maybes. Those who receive Jesus now have His promise of new life and eternal family. The proof? Jesus is alive! What more proof could (or should) God provide? We are to come willingly into His family in these Last Days, not unwillingly under compulsion in some future era. We can only come willingly *by faith* in this age, when we have faith *in the unseen* precisely because we do not have direct sight. Happy are they who have not seen and yet believed (John 20: 29).

To have faith now in absence of direct sight wins God's full and eternal

---

7 Your 'good works' will not suffice, nor will your religions. Jesus has done it all, on your behalf.
8 The command to repent is accompanied by urgent appeal to do it now. Paul quotes Isaiah 49:8, which speaks of *the day of salvation*. "I tell you, now is the time of God's favour. Now is the day of salvation" (2 Corinthians 6:2). Repentance should take place as soon as the Holy Spirit convicts us (John 16:8). In other words, **today is the day of salvation**. "Today, if only you would hear his voice, do not harden your hearts" (Psalm 95:7–8). Don't delay! No one knows the day he will die. After death comes judgment (Hebrews 9:27). The rich fool in Jesus' parable (Luke 12:16–20) thought he had plenty of time to enjoy life, but God had news for him: "This very night your life will be demanded from you" (verse 20). We have today, we have the present moment. We should use it wisely.

approval. Faith is always, and precisely, in Him Whom we cannot see, and yet in Whom we place our full trust even should it cost us our lives in this world. It is a willing family that God is building, not an unwilling one[9].

Signs – to look out for

Whilst we will resist the temptation to "map out" future events with precision and create a 'roadmap', as so many others have sought to do, we want to remain 100% focused on what the Bible actually says and about which there can be no (serious) argument. Chapter seven gives a good overall view of what we must look out for. In addition, Appendices 1 to 4 give more granular insight. These are the signs of the end time, and today we expect more and more of the 'warning lights' to progress from green, to amber and then to red – and to stay at red! Ultimately, readers must make up their own minds as to whether, and to what extent, these signs are occurring today; it may not be an exact science from our human perspective!

In Appendices 1 to 4 we provide schematic listings of the 'signs' of which the Bible forewarns. Readers are invited to ponder the RAG-status[10] of these signs in our own day, and of which (in their own view) remain stubbornly at 'red' in these our present days. This is a helpful exercise and allows us to engage with scripture seriously, but it is not 'an exact science' – and nor is it meant to be. Different readers will have different perspectives and there will never be universal agreement on these matters. Some critics may take issue with some of the 'signs' that we suggest (for example, on-demand *abortion*). Readers must, once again, make up their own minds on our Appendices 1 to 4 based upon the broad witness of Scripture, the specific words of Jesus and the nature (and attributes) of the God of Righteousness and Justice. Whilst universal agreement on the specifics of signs is unlikely, we do anticipate ultimate broad agreement amongst Bible-believing Christians.

---

9 This is one reason why the Roman Catholic belief in purgatory (punishment in an afterlife *earning* some sort of 'salvation') must be declared as both unscriptural and illogical. It is a *willing* family that is being assembled by God now and today, not a compelled 'family' of those who *have not* exercised faith, and *have* consciously rejected the offer of Life. The good news continues to be that repentance and restoration is possible for, and open to, all people everywhere in these Last Days.
10 RAG = Red, Amber, Green.

CHAPTER 6

SHOFAR BLASTS

**above all, you must understand that in the last days scoffers will come,
scoffing and following their own evil desires (2 Peter 3:3).**

Warning signals

Scripturally, the shofar (a ram's horn converted into a trumpet) was used as a method of proclamation or warning, as an alarm, or as an instrument of praise or prayer[1]. As we saw in our previous chapter, the festival of trumpets (or more correctly *shofarim*) is one of the seven Moeds celebrated by ancient Israel, and each Moed speaks prophetically of the life, mission and ministry of Jesus. In Matthew chapters 24 and 25 the Lord Jesus speaks of what we are to anticipate and look out for towards the end of the last days, which are in fact the beginning of the end times[2]. Furthermore there are to be many, many signals before the end comes and these are highlighted throughout Scripture.

We can say that, prophetically, the next 'item' on the *Jesus agenda* (if we may respectfully and reverently style it in that way) is "trumpets", or *shofarim*, given that today we are living in *the last days* as we defined them in chapter 1. It is tempting to try to map-out all the 'signs' of our proximity to the end, as we saw in chapter 5. Whilst there are clear clues given to us, yet a precise "roadmap" is what God - in His Wisdom - has chosen *not* to provide for us. Rather, we are called to read the signs but always to remember that, in the words of the apostle Paul, we are presently peering "through a glass darkly" (1 Corinthians 13:12 (AV)). In other words we have only a partial vision at this point. It is in this spirit and in clear acknowledgement that we do not have all the answers, that your author penned this chapter. We trust that readers will find it helpful.

---

1 Interested readers are encouraged to get Greg Stevenson's short booklet "The Message of the Shofar – And Its Application to Believers through the Feasts of The Lord" (Olive Tree Press, November 2010 and available from CMJ).
2 See chapter 1 for the distinction between the last days, and the end times.

As clear signs are scripturally prefigured and as many of these signs will occur with increasing frequency and urgency before the return of Yeshua ha Maschiasch (Jesus the Messiah), it is helpful to list them. That is what we seek to achieve in this chapter. Whilst the Bible gives many and varied signs, as we shall see in our next chapter, seven appear to stand out:

Nation Against Nation

In Matthew 24:7, Yeshua gives us one of the clear signs, saying that, "Nation will rise against nation, and kingdom against kingdom."

False Prophets

In Matthew 24:24, Jesus warns of another sign, saying "For false messiahs and false prophets will arise and perform great signs and wonders, so as to lead astray, if possible, even the elect."

But there is a way we can discern who is true from who is false. Yeshua says, in John 14:21, "Whoever has my commands and obeys them, he is the one who loves me. He who loves me will be loved by my Father, and I too will love him and show myself to him."

Moral Decay

In 2 Timothy 3:1-4, Paul writes of a sign: "But understand this, that in the last days there will come times of difficulty. For people will be lovers of self, lovers of money, proud, arrogant, abusive, disobedient to their parents, ungrateful, unholy, heartless, unappeasable, slanderous, without self-control, brutal, not loving good, treacherous, reckless, swollen with conceit, lovers of pleasure rather than lovers of God."

Since human beings have always reflected all of these vices, we must assume that these traits will occur at an unprecedented level – more brutal, more heartless, and more greedy and proud than ever.

The fall from God-inspired morality to relativity is a mark of the postmodern age. Ours is a society that has become suspicious of anything labelled "truth," and this may very well be the beginning of the particular sign of which Timothy is warned. Moral relativism allows for the creation of personal codes of morality, of personal interpretations of truth – everything is up to the individual. This may eventually allow for the extreme behaviours listed in this sign. If one word implies rebellion against God, it is perhaps the word 'pride'.

Remember the fruit of the spirit – love, joy, peace, forbearance, kindness, goodness, faithfulness, gentleness and self-control. Live by these, and we shall avoid the trap of moral decay into which, sadly, so many are destined to fall.

Signs in the Stars

In Luke 21:25-26, Messiah speaks of the sky, saying, "And there will be signs in sun and moon and stars, and on the earth distress of nations in perplexity because of the roaring of the sea and the waves, people fainting with fear and with foreboding of what is coming on the world. For the powers of the heavens will be shaken."

This commentary is one about which we cannot be definitive at this stage. It appears in several places in the Gospels. Other verses speak of "roaring" in the heavens, as well as some kind of tumult in the seas. However these predictions emerge, one thing is certain – this sign will be impossible to miss!

A Great Tribulation

The Great Tribulation[3] is another contentious sign. Some interpret surrounding scripture to mean that believers will be taken up into heaven and spared this difficult time. Others believe that they will not be taken up until after it (see our chapter 12 for further insights).

Of this time, Messiah Yeshua says "then there will be a great tribulation, such as has not occurred since the beginning of the world until now, nor ever shall." (Matthew 24: 2). This Tribulation will be initiated by an action of the Antichrist that will only conclude with the coming of the true Messiah.

Earthquakes in Many Places

Earthquakes play a big role in Biblical prophecy. In Matthew 24: 6-7, Yeshua says that "there will be famines and earthquakes in various places" when the time is near for His return. Notice the "various places." We cannot point to every earthquake that happens and think that the end is coming – this sign will be something different, something more widespread and much more intense. Like many of the signs, this is something we are familiar with, but will be greatly intensified. These will not be those 'run of the mill' earthquakes with which we are familiar. Rather, they will be something that will rock the very foundations of the earth, and do so in many places at once.

Earthquakes are mentioned five times in the Book of Revelation, with the final earthquake corresponding with the seventh bowl of God's wrath being poured out on the earth. This is described as "a great earthquake, such a mighty and great earthquake as had not occurred since men were on the earth. Now the great city was divided into three parts, and the cities of the nations fell."

This is another sign that will be difficult to miss, but we must take care to interpret it correctly. These signs are merely the "birth pains" of Yeshua's return, and even in these frightening times, there will be hope for a better world.

---

3 "Great distress" in the words of the NIV bible.

A universal, one world religion

In some sense, the character the Bible identifies as the Antichrist will set up a global religion. Revelation chapter 13 alludes to this. This religion will be anti-Christ; not only in the sense that it is directly opposed to Jesus (that goes without saying) but also in the sense that it is "instead of Christ". The late David Pawson reminds us that the term "antichrist" can be correctly read as "instead of Christ". The devil has no special interest in which religion people immerse themselves, providing it is *instead of* (or in place of) Messiah Jesus.

Be prepared

Yeshua tells us of the importance of these signs when He says, "From the fig tree learn its lesson: as soon as its branch becomes tender and puts out its leaves, you know that summer is near." Surely that is the essence as to why we have been forewarned of these signs – of these shofar blasts – so we might know that Messiah Jesus is near and take heart, and so that we might also prepare ourselves.

The shofar blast was always a signal to people that they were to be prepared and to 'assemble' before God. It remains God's gracious purpose to forewarn His chosen ones. The 'signs' we are exploring may of course be a catalyst for many individual people to place their trust and faith in Messiah Jesus. Yet far, far too many will 'hold out' to the bitter end, when time has run out, and refuse His offer of Life. We repeat, the one word that encapsulates mankind's rebellion against Jesus is 'pride' – and we know that *pride comes before destruction* (Proverbs 16: 18). Our next chapter helps us to explore the theme of Messiah's second coming in greater depth.

CHAPTER 7

THE SECOND COMING

*"Son of man," he said to me, "understand that
the vision concerns the time of the end." (Daniel 8:17).*

What do we mean by 'The Second Coming'?

Yeshua was clear that He will return physically to this world. The mechanism
and immediate results of this bodily return remain, even today, an area of
immense controversy amongst Christians. No wonder there is confusion
amongst non-Christians! Sometimes this controversy is deeply unhelpful
– your author would go so far as to say, it is demonically inspired – and of
course Christians should not be swayed by demonic forces! The doctrine of the
second coming, then, has tended to pit Christian against Christian. We need to
handle the teaching with great care! This chapter is in the form of an extended
thematic Bible study, and is borrowed with permission (and minor edits) from
the book "The Bible Student".[1]

What do we mean by The Second Coming? This is the visible return of
Yeshua, the Messiah, to this world. It is a still future event. Note that as this
chapter deals primarily with the future, so we should approach the subject
with a sense of caution, humility and reverence. We must recognise that
although the fact of Jesus' return is certain, it is unwise to be too dogmatic
about details. Greek words used in the Bible in reference to the Messiah's return
are "Parousia", "Apocaluqsis", "epithaneia", and others. *All imply a visible return.*

How do we know that there will be a visible return
of Jesus to His World?

The Old Testament clearly predicted the first coming of the Messiah, even
giving details of his death (see especially Isaiah 52 and 53). Yet the majority of

---

1 "The Bible Student", Christian Publications International, 2010.

the Hebrew nation was unprepared and blind to the things that were happening. The Bible is equally emphatic about Jesus' visible *return* – the second coming. Jesus Himself referred to His second coming more than 20 times, and there are more than 200 such references elsewhere in the New Testament. As Jesus fulfilled all the prophecies concerning the first coming of the Messiah contained in the Old Testament, so will He fulfil all prophesies relating to His second coming. See especially Acts **1**: 11 and 1 Thessalonians **4**: 14.

> Psalm **22**: 1, 7, 13 – 18
> Acts **1**: 11
> Matthew **24**: 21 – 30
> John **14**: 3
> Romans **11**: 25 – 26
> 1 Corinthians **1**: 7
> Philippians **3**: 20 – 21
> 1 Thessalonians **1**: 9 – 10; **2**: 19; **3**: 12 – 13; **4**: 16, 18
> Titus **2**: 13
> Hebrews **9**: 28

Before His return, certain things will have happened:

A long time will pass after the first coming. Time is relative and is not a "problem" for God, but it is a problem for humans!

> Matthew **24**: 6 – 8, 48
> Matthew **25**: 5, 19

Note that the scriptures emphasise the absolute necessity of being prepared for Christ's return at any moment – and of course He may return for any one of us, individually, at any moment! We are each one of us but a heartbeat from eternity!

The Hebrew people will be preserved as a nation in dispersion. At the time of the end, they will return to the land that God promised to them. This is happening.

> Deuteronomy **30**: 3
> Isaiah **11**: 10 – 12
> Isaiah **60**: 9
> Jeremiah **30**: 11, 18; **31**: 10 – 13
> Ezekiel **36**: 24 – 36; **37**: 1 – 11

Luke **21**: 24 (many consider that the time of the Gentiles has now ended)
Romans **11**: 25 (there will be an increasing turning among Jewish people to their Lord – Yeshua (the Hebrew name for Jesus))

The gospel of Jesus must have been proclaimed across the entire world. This again has now virtually happened, and increasingly so through the internet. Although not completely fulfilled, this emphasises the urgency of missionary work.

Mark **16**: 15
Matthew **24**: 14

Many false religions will arise – some in the name of Jesus. Religions will be marked out by their refusal to acknowledge the deity of Jesus, the truth of His propitiatory death on the cross, or the truth of His resurrection from death. Some sects and religions will align themselves with what may be called normative Christianity (e.g. the Russellites, Christadelphians, Christian Scientists, Mormons etc) although it must be noted that the very term "Christian" is now inadequate to truly describe the disciples of Jesus. There will be a new emphasis on aligning the religions and preaching that ultimately they are all one, under God. This is a heresy, but will be encountered more and more in the future, even within "churches".

Matthew **24**: 5, 11, 24
Luke **17**: 23
2 Peter **2**: 1 – 2
2 Thessalonians **2**: 3

The times of the Gentiles must have run its course – Gentile domination of Jerusalem and the ancient lands of Israel will end – Luke **21**: 24.

Birth Pangs – Jesus described the approach of His return as being like *birth pangs*. The pangs arise so we know that something is about to happen. Jesus' explanation of the future is contained in Matthew chapter 24, which you may want to pause and read in its entirety.

At the time of His return, certain things will be happening:

Unprecedented calamities – earthquakes and associated societal dislocations. Political crises. Godlessness. Persecution of the true followers of Jesus, whether they are Jewish or Gentile. These will be unprecedented in the sense that their intensity will increase, there will be more of them, and they will happen together.

Daniel **12:** 9 – 10
Joel **2:** 31
Zephaniah **1:** 14 – 18
Matthew **24:** 9 – 10, 21
Luke **21:** 11, 25
2 Timothy **3:** 1 – 5

Organised Christianity will be absorbed into the World. There will be global apostasy – a turning away from Christ to other things. Christian "religion" will become in different ways cold, formal, asleep, or aligned to other religions. Sadly, the so-called "church" will be as unprepared for *The Second Coming* as the Hebrew religious leaders were for the *first* coming. In both cases the religious leaders should have been alert and aware. In the past they were not. In the future (present?) they apparently are not.

Matthew **24:** 3 – 4, 9, 12, 24, 44
Matthew **25:** 1 – 13
Luk**e 17:** 26 – 27**, 30; 18:** 8**; 21**: 34 – 35
Mark **13:** 36
1 Thessalonians **5:** 1 – 6
2 Peter **3:** 3 – 4
Revelation **3:** 15 – 18

There will be a worldwide fear for the future

Luke **21:** 25 – 26

Some believers will be expecting His return. There will be a hidden remnant that will be ready, waiting and scattered across the world, from all races.

Daniel **12:** 9 – 10
Matthew **25:** 1 – 3, 8
Luke **21:** 35 – 36

There will have been a return to Israel of Jewish people on a large scale.

> Isaiah **11:** 11 – 12
> Ezekiel **37:** 11, 14, 21 – 22

A global dictator and religious leader will appear. It appears he will arise in Europe, but we should not be dogmatic about the location. He will gain worldwide power. He will be religiously followed – and feared. After being victorious he will have designs upon Israel. This leader may be aligned with, or may be identical to, the apostate leader of a reunited "Christendom" – The Anti-Messiah. This person may be the ultimate architect of a harmonised religion, or out of the religions he may form a new, final religion.

> Daniel **7:** 8 (the 'little horn' is the **Anti-Christ**)
> Daniel **11:** 36 – 45
> Daniel **12 :** 1
> Matthew **24:** 14 – 16
> 2 Thessalonians **2:** 3 – 12
> Revelation **13:** 3 – 18; **19:** 17 – 20

Again we emphasise in relation to the immediate preceding material that it is unprofitable to be too dogmatic about the details, but the general outline is plain to see – there will be a global politico-religious leader/ship that is in opposition to Christ – and ultimately this will be destroyed by Christ.

The world will be in the throes of a final great war. This will be a war ultimately against God, involving the Jewish people in some way, and centred on the land of Israel. This is called Armageddon. Israel will be seen as defenceless. Many Jewish people will turn to Jesus (Yeshua) as their Messiah, because of the great distress at that time. But the Lord will have the final word in this. The enemy will not prevail.

> Ezekiel **38:** 8 – 12, 15, 21 – 22
> Joel **3:** 1 – 2, 9 – 11, 14
> Zechariah **12:** 1 – 10; **14:** 1 – 9
> Romans **11:** 26 – 27
> Revelation **16:** 14, 16

<u>Note</u>: some argue that elements of these prophecies have already passed. Overall this seems not to be the case. But *some* prophecies certainly did have both a short-term outworking, and a second longer-term outworking[2]. Some of the prophecies referred to in this study will be in this *short-long* term category. The short-term outworking would have been in biblical times, but the future outworking is still awaited.

The actual coming of the Lord:

There are a number of interpretations of what the Bible says. We would again caution against being overly or destructively-divisively dogmatic about this. What we can say is that **the return will be visible, dramatic and definitive**. It will be a surprise to the World at large – and to many in the church, it seems. As the apostle Paul wrote, to most it will come *like a thief in the night* (1 Thessalonians **5**: 2 – 4). No one expects a thief, or they would be ready for him!

The purpose of the second coming is to glorify the Lord – and His true Church, His bride – His 'called-out' ones from all nations, races and tongues – now at last triumphant. The precise details are somewhat mysterious but most Bible-believing Christians would generally recognise the following:

Jesus/Yeshua's disciples will be called in some visible, separate way
1 Corinthians **15:** 51 – 53
1 Thessalonians **4:** 13 – 17
Luke **17:** 24, 34 – 36
(Please see this book, Chapter 12 for further insights).

The Lord's physical return is clear
1 Thessalonians **3:** 13
Zechariah **14:** 4 – 5

The Second Coming
Matthew **24:** 27 – 31, 39
Matthew **25:** 6, 13, 31 – 23
Luke **12:** 39 – 40; **21:** 27 – 28, 34 – 35
Acts **1:** 7, 10 – 11
Colossians **3:** 4
1 Peter **5:** 4
1 John **2:** 28

---

2   See Appendix 6 for further insights into this subject.

A period of Messiah's rule on earth
Revelation **20:** 1 – 4
Isaiah **11:** 6 – 9
Jeremiah **23:** 5 – 6
Zechariah **14:** 9
(Please see this book, Chapter 13 for further insights).

The end:

The destruction of evil, the judgment, and the end of the present earth
Revelation **20:** 7 – 10
Hebrews **1:** 10 – 12
2 Peter **3:** 10 – 13
Revelation **20:** 11 – 14

A New Heaven and a New Earth
Revelation **21:** 1, 4
1 Corinthians **15:** 24 – 28

Final prayer – Revelation **22:** 20 "Amen. Come Lord Yeshua"

CHAPTER 8

WHERE SCRIPTURE IS OBSCURE

**many will be purged, cleansed, and refined, but the wicked will act
wickedly. And none of the wicked will understand, but those who have
insight will understand (Daniel 12:10).**

Hidden

We have noted already that Jesus is sometimes "hidden in plain sight" in terms
of the 'types' and 'shadows' of Messiah contained in the Old Testament, and in
the picture language contained in the book of Revelation in the New Testament.
The interconnectedness and consistency of Scripture continues to amaze, even
today! Ultimately, it is all about Jesus – there is no theme greater than Messiah
Yeshua in the Bible. We must be candid and honest, however, and acknowledge
that in some places, particularly in terms of the *end time* events, Scripture
provides both direct and indirect allusions which can be difficult to trace
through. We do not suggest any inconsistency in the revelation of the Holy Spirit,
but we do acknowledge obscurity in some areas, *which is surely God's intention*.
God chooses to keep some things obscure. In God's economy we might say
that 'now is not the right time for full understanding'. In other words God will
choose His time to make things crystal clear, and that will be when we need such
knowledge, rather than to satisfy our (sometimes) idle curiosity.

As we acknowledged in the preceding chapter (#7) there are places in
Scripture where understandings (interpretations) vary amongst true Believers. It
seems that God has given us some degree of latitude in insight and interpretation,
providing that such 'interpretation' does not run counter to the clear directives of
Scripture. Hence it would be foolish to suggest that Scripture can be 'interpreted'
to mean, for example, that the Resurrection, or indeed the penal substitution
of Messiah Jesus, does not mean what Scripture plainly teaches. The theologies
of e.g. the Jehovah's Witnesses and the Mormons must be pronounced as false,
irrespective of any sincerity with which their beliefs may be held. The 'theologies'
of some of "liberal Christian" persuasion must, by the same token, also be
pronounced untrue. So- called 'liberation theology' would be a case in point.

Beware of *eisegesis* (a reading-into scripture what you want to find, or indeed expect to find). Aim for *exegesis* wherever possible – and that means in 98% of cases – as this is the normative way of exploring and understanding Scripture. Exegesis is to 'read-out' of Scripture what is plainly there.

Regarding this eisegesis versus exegesis dichotomy, we would comment that CPI's book "The Bible Student" represents good exegetical insight, and we commend it on that basis. It covers some fifty key Bible themes as areas of interest to all Christians, and it generally follows its various themes from the Old Testament and into the New to give an over-arching understanding of how God speaks on these subjects. The book is freely available in down-loadable PDF format, as well as sold in traditional 'paperback' format. Visit the CPI website for more information.

In stating that Scripture is in some places obscure, we are obviously saying that in other places it is crystal clear. The previous two chapters (# 6 and 7) explored areas where Scripture is reasonably clear, especially if we approach it with humility and expectancy. Where Scripture remains unclear, we need to tread with caution and avoid divisive dogmatism. UK writer David Pawson in his magisterial work "Unlocking the Bible" makes the useful point that in 'interpreting' Scripture we need to be aware of the differences between "Hebraic" and "Greek" thinking. He notes also that chapter and verse numbers in the Bible (not part of the original text) can interfere with a natural reading of the text and can, in some places, be influenced by the theologians' preconceived ideas. Pawson states this in relation to the book of Revelation, but the principle remains true elsewhere in the Bible. Chapter and verse numbering is not always helpful!

With regard to Greek versus Hebraic thinking, this is a massive subject in its own right. Contemporary UK writer Steve Maltz has done more in the past ten years to explore these powerful thought-engines than any other theologian, and we particularly recommend several of his books – see note at end of this paragraph* and the further reading section at the end of this book for full details. Maltz is highly recommended in his own right but especially as this subject of Hebraic versus Greek thinking is so pervasive, yet so little understood.[1] Your authors encourage our readers to independently explore

---

1 In negotiation training in the business world, students are encouraged to understand their personal "style" of personality traits, as well as recognising such traits in others, because these traits can be a powerful factor in determining the outcome of negotiation encounters. 'Hebraic' versus 'Greek' mindsets are similarly powerful indicators of how people will read, interpret and apply Scripture – yet most Christians remain blissfully unaware of these differences. They similarly fail to perceive that the Bible is largely a Hebraic text and needs to be understood, to a large extent, with a clear acknowledgment of the text's Hebraic root - what did the original writer mean, how would the original readers have understood, and how do we reapply today?

this important subject as it seems that God is today graciously 'reminding' Christians that *the root is vitally important* and *where the root suffers, so the whole body is damaged*. We ignore these truths at our spiritual peril!

* Hebraic Church (Maltz)
* Livin' the Life (Maltz)
* Shalom (Maltz)
* Into the Lion's Den (Maltz)
* The Sinner's Charter (Maltz)
* To Life! (Maltz)

Obscure?

What your author here describes as obscure, others may well style as completely transparent and indeed hold their views both doggedly and dogmatically. We can say with little controversy that the book of Revelation 'reveals' the future and that this New Testament book is intimately interconnected with others texts, but especially the books Ezekiel, Daniel and Zechariah from the Old Testament. An understanding of how these texts interrelate is helpful in appreciating the broad scheme of end time events. Note, incidentally, we are here making the clear point that they deal principally with *end time*, rather than *last days* truths[2].

Many Christians struggle with the Old Testament prophets. There are quite a few! Some are described as 'minor' and some are 'major', depending on length. They often seem repetitive and archaic. Can they really speak to us today? Some Christians will say that we really need be concerned primarily with the New Testament and the Old should be relegated or delegated to specialists. These people will often add that it is the purported "love" of God that is to be celebrated, and they think the Old Testament fails adequately to reveal this "love". Such Christians miss out tremendously in their understanding, insights and exegetical power – and lay themselves open to spiritual attack, and defeat. Jesus Himself confirmed that he had not come to challenge the Law (that is, the Old Testament) but to fulfill it (Matthew 5: 17). He added that not 'one jot or tittle' (in the words of the old AV translation) of the Law would pass away until ALL has been fulfilled (Matthew 5: 18). Since much of Old Testament prophecy lies yet in our future, we must conclude that it remains an essential reading for all true disciples, and where it seems

---

2 Refer again to chapters 1 to 3 of this book.

'difficult' we must faithfully work through those 'difficulties' to understand what God is saying to us today.

We can however, make some easy inroads into the Old Testament prophets when we recognise something simple that certainly does not leap off the page at us, but rather needs to be pointed out! There were two traumatic events in the Old Testament that have resonance today and have resonance in the lives of individual believers. Those two events were the conquest of Israel by Assyria in 722 BC and by Babylonia in 587 BC. Politically, these defeats might be explained by the sheer power of Israel's bigger neighbours. Spiritually, these defeats are solely attributable to Israel's dalliance with pagan religions and serial rebellion against the one true God, as the *Chosen People* continually broke His laws. For the individual Believer today, we face our own often terrifying 'neighbours' in the shape of the World, the Flesh and the Devil. To survive against, and ultimately defeat, these enemies we need to remain true to our Saviour God and to His clear commands. Compromise leads to defeat.

> *Readers may want at this point to refer to the schematic map*
> *printed in the back inside cover. It reminds us, in basic terms,*
> *of those two traumatic exiles from the lands of Israel.*

The various and sometimes confusing Old Testament prophets can be easily divided into two camps; those who prophesied the Assyrian defeat and those who foretold the Babylonian defeat. Our schematic referenced immediately above summarises this[3]. The Assyrian defeat led to the so-called ten tribes of Israel being taken **north** in the first national exile. The later Babylon defeat saw the Judean Jews exiled progressively in an **east**erly direction to Babylon. The Babylonian exile resulted in an eventual return of many Jews to their promised land and Israel essentially continued, albeit in a chastened and reduced form.[4] In terms of our focus in this book, we are interested in those prophecies that allude to the End Times, and this is where things can get rather confusing and where God's purposes can be obscure. We would go so far as to say that the truths of these prophecies and their spiritual interconnectedness are fully

---

3 We think reasonably accurately, but note there is inevitably scholastic debate about timings, dating and even authorship. The view expressed in our schematic is the broadly accepted view.
4 A third and more profound exile from the lands was at the hands of the Roman Empire in the First Century AD. Whilst this is certainly alluded to in the Old Testament (see again chapter 4) there is far less focus on this third exile in Scripture. It occurred, in any case, after the books of the New Testament were written, and in that sense, after the canon of Scripture was closed.

discernible only to the eyes of faith via the inspiration of the Holy Spirit. So, for example, these truths will not be revealed to UK's professor Richard Dawkins![5] Sadly the World at large will continue in its hatred of, and in its rejection of, God's ultimate end-time purpose for Israel. Similarly the World will continue in its determined rejection of God's laws, summarised in the Ten Commandments. In that sense, the World is on a collision course with its Creator God, and that collision can have only one outcome.

This book is not a dedicated commentary on particular Old or New Testament books. Such insights are generally amassed over a lifetime of study, so your author makes no apology that we make some sweeping generalisations and do not always seek to defend these to the "nth degree"! We commend again David Pawson's significant "Unlocking the Bible" as a unique and intelligent, yet eminently readable, commentary on every Bible book. We can say, however, that some elements of the Scriptures enjoy greater common agreement amongst scholars, theologians and Berean Christians than others. In other words these are less controversial! With regard to *the end time* there is huge controversy, even amongst Berean Christians (perhaps especially amongst Berean Christians!) as to how the varying texts interrelate and precisely how we are to understand them.

Our key point here is that in some places we can be sure we fully understand texts as they relate to the future. In other places we can be reasonably sure. Yet in others we must exercise some real humility and admit that the truth has not yet been fully revealed to us. In the words of the apostle Paul, we presently *look through a glass darkly* (1 Corinthians 13: 12, AV). In the Table below we offer a snapshot (no more) of the sorts of areas where we can be certain, where reasonably sure and where we must acknowledge that, although God is on the move, yet so far He has declined to provide for us a clear 'roadmap' of His intentions. We repeat something said earlier in this book; in terms of God's eschatological purposes, some things are frankly none of our business! We need to be honest with ourselves, and with others who may be truth seekers, that this is the case. We need a little humility in this . . .

---

5 At the time of writing, Richard Dawkins is known and celebrated by the secular media as a died-in the-wool prophet of the modern religion of atheism. Clever, he may be, but spiritual truth eludes him as these things must be spiritually discerned. So we are of the decided opinion that Richard Dawkins presently could have no insight or understanding of end-times, nor indeed any other matter that is determined by the Holy Spirit.

SPECTRUM OF END TIME UNDERSTANDING

SURE	REASONABLY SURE	SPECULATIVE
Jesus' return	Unprecedented calamities ('tribulation')	Rise of China
Jesus' return to Jerusalem	Christian apostasy (widespread)	AI linked to mark of the beast system
Long time	Widespread fear across planet Earth	EU as revived Roman Empire
False religions	Expectancy	Role of Turkey
Antichrist	The Beast	The two witnesses
= Broad agreement/ consensus	= Broad agreement among those who seek diligently	= Not for now!

The basic thinking behind the above is explored more fully in Chapter 7.

The Babylon Theme

Babylon (or Babylonia) was an ancient kingdom that flourished in southern Mesopotamia, especially in the 7th and 6th centuries BC. Its capital city was Babylon (or Bab-ilu, meaning 'gate of god'). Babylon was an overwhelmingly powerful enemy in the context of Israel and would defeat Israel comprehensively in 587 BC. Babylon, however, in spite of being a geopolitical reality – and an extremely brutal culture – would also become a powerful statement or symbol of all those things opposed to the true Creator God. In other words it was, and remains today, a powerful spiritual motif. If Zion is the motif for the city of God, so Babylon is the motif for opposition to God.

In the New Testament, as God ushers in His Kingdom under a 'new covenant', Babylon is used symbolically. "She who is at Babylon" was the apostle Peter's way of referring to the church in Rome – a city that was as idolatrous and immoral as was ancient Babylon. Just as that ancient cultural centre had oppressed the Judean exiles, so Rome would oppress the Christian believers who lived there. At the end of the Bible, in Revelation 14:8, 16:19, 17:5, and 18:2,10 and 21, Babylon is again used as a symbol of first-century Rome. It was pictured as "the notorious prostitute, who sits on many waters". Gorgeously arrayed like a queen, she sits on a scarlet beast with seven heads and ten horns, "drunk with the blood of the saints". On her forehead is written "Babylon the great, mother of harlots and of earth's abominations" (17:1-6). The wickedness of Babylon is clearly an oblique reference to the evils of first-century Rome.

Revelation 18 becomes the climax and end of spiritual Babylon of the future. Note that some Christian commentators consider the Western World to be Babylon. Others consider all the World's political and social structures (including religions) diametrically opposed to God's revealed purposes, as being Babylon. There may be more than one legitimate interpretation. "**Fallen, fallen is Babylon the Great**" (18:2). God's final judgment on her will be severe, repaying her "**double for her deeds**" (18:6). The key reason for her downfall is her immorality and her persecution of the saints (19:2). The kings and merchants of the world mourn her downfall (18: 9-19), but the pronouncement is made so that the saints might rejoice and worship God.[6]

What can we say about Babylon in the context of Scriptures that may be obscure? Firstly we can clarify what is broadly accepted historical fact. Our schematic in the inside back cover cites the key prophets and their prophetic connection with both Assyria and Babylon. As regards the main elements of the Babylon exiles, we know there were three deportations and essentially three homecomings for the children of Israel:

Three deportations . . .

a) 606 BC	(elite / top layer)	
b) 597	(upper classes)	
c) 586	(population at large)	(Temple destroyed)

---

6 George Frideric Handel's *Hallelujah Chorus* of his *Messiah* oratorio is often thought to be part of the "Christmas" celebrations. In fact it is the saints crying out *Hallelujah* in joy when the evil power structures of this world come crashing down – see Revelation chapter 19. Perhaps people would be less comfortable with Handel's *Hallelujah Chorus* if they really understood it's true meaning! This is an online article by Peter Sammons on Handel's Messiah: https://christiancomment.org/2021/01/19/handel-the-messiah/

Three returns . . .

538 BC	(Persians defeat Babylonians)
458	(Ezra)
444	(walls rebuilt (Nehemiah))

That much is of historical record, albeit fine details may be disputed by scholars. The exile to Babylon was a huge spiritual, political and social blow to Israel and, unsurprisingly, many Jews never returned to Israel as they put down roots and often assimilated with their new de-facto host society. From the words of Jesus we can understand end time realities (see Matthew chapter 24 and Luke chapter 21 in particular.) Via other prophecies we can say, as we summarise in our schematic below, that in our future lots of 'stuff will happen' in the sense of major events and issues emerging, and that Israel will very often have a central role. Towards the very end there will be a time of distress (called the Tribulation or "big trouble" in David Pawson's words) both for the world at large and in particular for Jewish people and for Christians. But eventually Jesus will return to commence what is called by some theologians His Millennial Rule[7]:

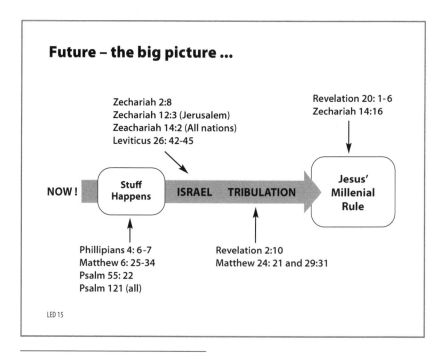

Future – the big picture ...

Zechariah 2:8
Zechariah 12:3 (Jerusalem)
Zeachariah 14:2 (All nations)
Leviticus 26: 42-45

Revelation 20: 1-6
Zechariah 14:16

NOW ! Stuff Happens ISRAEL TRIBULATION Jesus' Millenial Rule

Phillipians 4: 6-7
Matthew 6: 25-34
Psalm 55: 22
Psalm 121 (all)

Revelation 2:10
Matthew 24: 21 and 29:31

LED 15

---

7 Note that the terms 'Millennial Rule' and 'Millennium' are not found in the Bible. These are theological constructs. See chapter 13 of this book for further insights.

In terms of *last days* and *end time* (and especially in relation to end times) it is well enough understood that the book of Revelation, which prophesies the end in detail, is intimately interconnected with three major prophets – Daniel, Ezekiel and Zechariah. The relationship between these four books is intimate but difficult to trace; once again there is debate about precisely how these prophecies interrelate.

In a further schematic below ("Babylon and Revelation"), we make some generalisations and hope that these will help our readers to get a 'broad brush' insight into the key themes developed:

Babylon and Revelation

Daniel (7-12)

Four visions:
a) Four beasts (7: 1-28)
b) Ram and goat (8:1 - 9:27)
c) Heavenly messenger (10:1 - 11:45)
d) End time (12: 1-13)

Ezekiel (40-48)

God's judgement on the nations (25:1-32: 32)
Prophecy against Gog (38:1 – 39: 29)
Vision of future Temple and Land (40:1 - 48:35)

Zechariah (12-14)

Judgement on Israel's neighbours (9:1-8)
Future prosperity and peace (9:9 – 14: 21)

Revelation

Destruction of Babylon, defeat of 'the Beast', 'False Prophet' and devil. (17:1 - 20:10)
Final judgement (20:11-15),
New heaven, New earth (21:1 - 22:5)

LED 16

In Daniel there are four visions, and it is the last of these that concerns the end of this world. Ezekiel foresees God's judgment on the nations, both for their Babylon-like rebellion, but also on account of their specific warring against Israel. Finally Zechariah foretells the specific judgment on Israel's neighbours. For all their 'gloom and doom' these three prophets clearly foresee the Messiah. Daniel foresees the Messiah as God's heavenly messenger, Ezekiel perceives Him in the future Temple, and Zechariah in that future time of eternal peace and prosperity. Christians understand these prophecies, of course, as highlighting Messiah Yeshua (Jesus) and of His 'tabernacling' with His chosen people throughout eternity. As a shorthand of that last idea, we can say (incorrectly but at least understandably) that we shall live with our Saviour 'in heaven' forever.

The foregoing summary is extremely broad-brush, and of course there are specific questions to be engaged with in true Berean style, but we think it helps to bring some clarity where there may be obscurity . Babylon is the unifying symbol of all that opposes a holy, righteous and yet merciful and loving Creator God. No wonder we see Babylon throughout Scripture, from beginning to end, albeit it may have other code-names elsewhere in the Bible. At the time this book was being prepared, UK author David Lambourn had just completed his excellent "***Babel versus Bible***". We recommend this as an excellent way to understand, in a more rounded sense, the spiritual implications of Babel and how Babel operates today.

It is rightly said that Christians think rather too much about the past and not enough about the future. Our final schematic here poses the question in visual form; *where does God want our focus to be?*

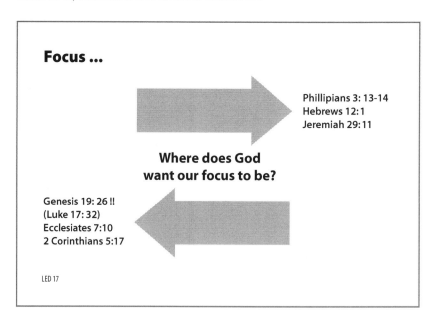

Focus ...

Phillipians 3: 13-14
Hebrews 12: 1
Jeremiah 29: 11

**Where does God
want our focus to be?**

Genesis 19: 26 !!
(Luke 17: 32)
Ecclesiates 7:10
2 Corinthians 5:17

LED 17

Yes, of course we have to think about the past. Our faith is rooted in historical truths and realities. Yes, we must think on and rejoice over our Saviour's incarnation, and of His crucifixion, resurrection and ascension. All these things are vitally important and lie in the past. But so too is the future vitally important. Jesus has gone out of His way (if we can reverently put it thus) to tell us what we should expect in terms of the end times. Today, those end times seem palpably to be drawing closer. As Jesus said, "**when you hear of these things, lift up your heads as you know your redemption draws near**" (Luke 21: 28).

Time to lift up our heads?

CHAPTER 9

MATTHEW CHAPTER 24

**at that time your people – everyone whose name
is found written in the book – will be delivered (Daniel 12:1).**

Jesus sets the terms for the future

It is in Matthew chapter 24 – and its counterpart in Luke chapter 21 – that we get Jesus' clear directive of what we are to expect at the end. In this chapter of our book we shall use large extracts from both Bible chapters. These extracts, below, are taken from the online *Berean Study Bible*, as a useful and broadly literal modern English translation. Readers can easily compare and contrast with their own preferred translation. The headings are added by the Berean Bible's editors, not being a part of the original text. Your author's comments are below each extract:

Temple Destruction and Other Signs
(Mark 13:1–8; Luke 21:5–9)

1 As Jesus left the temple and was walking away, His disciples came up to Him to point out its buildings. **2** "Do you see all these things?" He replied. "Truly I tell you, not one stone here will be left on another. Every one will be thrown down." **3** While Jesus was sitting on the Mount of Olives, the disciples came to Him privately. "Tell us," they said, "when will these things happen, and what will be the sign of Your coming and of the end of the age?" **4** Jesus answered, "See to it that no one **deceives** you. **5** For many will come in My name, claiming, 'I am the Christ,' and will **deceive** many. **6** You will hear of wars and rumours of wars, but see to it that you are not alarmed. These things must happen, but the end is still to come. **7** Nation will rise against nation, and kingdom against kingdom. There will be famines and earthquakes in various places. **8** All these are the beginning of birth pains.

AUTHOR COMMENT:

Here Jesus seems to be referring in two timeframes. First He prophesies the destruction of the Jerusalem Temple, which happened in AD70.

But Jesus' call to be aware of, and wary towards, falsehood and the claiming of Messiahship seems to cover all of the Last Days as we have defined that period in this book.

From the earliest times of the Christian era there have been periodic arisings of people who claim to be Messiah. But we are to be wary, they are never what they claim to be.

Witnessing to All Nations

(Mark 13:9–13; Luke 21:10–19)

9 Then they will deliver you over to be persecuted and killed, and you will be hated by all nations because of My name. **10** At that time many will fall away and will betray and hate one another, **11** and many false prophets will arise and **mislead** many. **12** Because of the multiplication of wickedness, the love of most will grow cold. **13** But the one who perseveres to the end will be saved. **14** And this gospel of the kingdom will be preached in all the world as a testimony to all nations, and then the end will come.

AUTHOR COMMENT:

Here Jesus anticipates two things, again in two different timeframes. First is the early persecution which started even in the book of Acts. Yet this persecution grows global, as the gospel itself is faithfully preached across planet earth. Is there any place on Earth today that has not heard the good news of Jesus?

The Abomination of Desolation

(Mark 13:14–23; Luke 21:20–24)

15 So when you see standing in the holy place 'the abomination of desolation,' described by the prophet Daniel (let the reader understand), **16** then let those who are in Judea flee to the mountains. **17** Let no one on the housetop come down to retrieve anything from his house. **18** And let no one in the field return for his cloak. **19** How miserable those days will be for pregnant and nursing mothers! **20** Pray that your flight will not occur in the winter or on the Sabbath. **21** For at that time there will be great tribulation, unmatched from the beginning of the world until now, and never to be seen again. **22** If those days had not been cut short, nobody would be saved. But for the sake of the elect, those days will be cut short. **23** At that time, if anyone says to you, 'Look, here is the Christ!' or 'There He is!' **do not believe it**. **24** For false Christs and false prophets will appear and perform great signs and wonders that would **deceive** even the elect, if that were possible. **25** See, I have told you in advance.

> **AUTHOR COMMENT:**
>
> Once again, two timeframes are revealed simultaneously. The Roman legions in AD70 would have been considered as an abomination as they warred their way through the precincts of the Temple – even invading the 'holy of holies'.
>
> But there is a future outworking, which seems to be the Antichrist or the Beast, which pronounces itself as God. This event yet lies yet in our future.

The Return of the Son of Man
(Mark 13:24–27; Luke 21:25–28)

26 So if they tell you, 'There He is in the wilderness,' do not go out; or, 'Here He is in the inner rooms,' **do not believe** it. **27** For just as the lightning comes from the east and flashes as far as the west, so will be the coming of the Son of Man. **28** Wherever there is a carcass, there the vultures will gather. **29** Immediately after the tribulation of those days: 'The sun will be darkened, and the moon will not give its light; the stars will fall from the sky, and the powers of the heavens will be shaken.' **30** At that time the sign of the Son of Man will appear in heaven, and all the tribes of the earth will mourn. They will see the Son of Man coming on the clouds of heaven, with power and great glory. **31** And He will send out His angels with a loud trumpet call, and they will gather His elect from the four winds, from one end of the heavens to the other.

> **AUTHOR COMMENT:**
>
> Finally, Jesus will return. Whilst all through history (as we saw in chapter two) there have been times when Christians have wondered openly – *is this the time*? Yet we are told not to be deceived. There have been false Messiahs – and there will be in the future as well.
>
> But when Jesus returns, everyone will know about it! And the world at large will not be happy to finally see the Saviour, now coming in glory, majesty and power.

The Lesson of the Fig Tree
(Mark 13:28–31; Luke 21:29–33)

32 Now learn this lesson from the fig tree: As soon as its branches become tender and sprout leaves, you know that summer is near. **33** So also, when you see all these things, you will know that He is near, right at the door. **34** Truly I tell

you, this generation will not pass away until all these things have happened.
35 Heaven and earth will pass away, but My words will never pass away.

AUTHOR COMMENT:

We need to be aware of the signs. In reality these signs are shofar blasts, warning the faithful that times are changing.

The reference to "this generation" is the subject of much discussion. There is, in a sense, a truism that *the first generation of Christians saw many of these things happen.* They even saw the outpouring of the Holy Spirit, which might be likened to the "return" of Jesus. Yet Jesus, of course, has not yet come in glory and that first generation has long since departed.

Perhaps as Jesus speaks of "this generation" He is speaking of all those generations of believers who live in these 'last days'?

The sign of the fig tree?

In the Old Testament the people of Israel are sometimes represented as figs on a fig tree (Hosea 9:10, Jeremiah 24), or as a fig tree that bears no fruit (Jeremiah 8:13). In Micah 4:4 the age of the Messiah is pictured as one in which each man would sit under his fig tree without fear.

Some commentators understand this as an allusion to the recreation of the State of Israel (May 1948) and to the sprouting of leaves as new life in an old, dead tree. Others suggest that Jesus is saying that the signs should be easy enough to read by virtue of world events.

Readiness at Any Hour

(Genesis 6:1–7; Mark 13:32–37; Luke 12:35–48)

36 No one knows about that day or hour, not even the angels in heaven, nor the Son, but only the Father. **37** As it was in the days of Noah, so will it be at the coming of the Son of Man. **38** For in the days before the flood, people were eating and drinking, marrying and giving in marriage, up to the day Noah entered the ark. **39** And they were oblivious, until the flood came and swept them all away. So will it be at the coming of the Son of Man. **40** Two men will be in the field: one will be taken and the other left. **41** Two women will be grinding at the mill: one will be taken and the other left. **42** Therefore keep watch, because you do not know the day on which your Lord will come. **43** But understand this: If the homeowner had known in which watch of the night the thief was coming, he would have kept watch and would not have let his house be broken into. **44** For this reason, you also must be ready, because the Son of Man will come at an hour you do not expect. **45** Who then is the faithful and wise servant, whom the master has put in charge of his household, to give the others their food at the proper time? **46** Blessed is that servant whose master finds him doing so when he returns. **47** Truly I tell you, he will put him in charge of all his possessions. **48** But suppose that servant is wicked and says in his heart, 'My master will be away a long time.' **49** And he begins to beat his fellow servants and to eat and drink with drunkards. **50** The master of that servant will come on a day he does not expect and at an hour he does not anticipate. **51** Then he will cut him to pieces and assign him a place with the hypocrites, where there will be weeping and gnashing of teeth.

AUTHOR COMMENT:

Quite simply, the world at large will not be ready, in spite of the increasing tempo and volume of the signs (shofar blasts) that God sends.

At some point Christians will be miraculously taken from this world. It appears that this will be either at the end of the Tribulation period, or half way through. Cogent arguments can be made for both outcomes.

We think it less likely that Christians will be "whisked away" before the Tribulation. There are too many indicators that we shall suffer alongside the rest of the world, and indeed that we shall be persecuted until He comes in glory.

Verses 48-51 seem to suggest an apostate and rebellious 'church'.

In the above we can "see" that the time before Jesus' return will involve major ambiguities (including the love of most growing cold – 24:12 – which seems to include much of the conventionally professing 'church') and major troubles and difficulties within the world in its final rebellion against its Creator God. How sad! But we have been told about this ahead of time by our Lord Yeshua, so in reality there are, or should be, no surprises in what He has foretold.

Incidentally, this scenario rather underscores the foolishness of those theological theories that somehow the Church will triumph and lead this world back to its God. The technical term for this belief system is *dominionism*, and your author rejects this particular theology alongside the other popular theologies about the future. The truth is likely to be both more wonderful and more straightforward than many commentators allow for. If we may summarise; the world will continue to be in rebellion against God, and therefore lost in its own cesspit of sin until that time when the Lord returns. Then the world shall bow the knee to Him, whether or not they like it or want to (Revelation 20: 1-4). The time of final rebellion against God is marked out as a time of rampant pride, as 'Babylon' tries to erect its 'tower' to the heavenlies.

Lessons for today

As we look at Matthew chapter 24 (as indeed we read any biblical passage) we note it is not "hanging in the air" in isolation. It is set in a context, so let us look at that context for a moment. The Lord's time in this world is physically drawing to a close – His appointment with the Cross is now just weeks away. It's as if the tempo of teaching is being ramped-up by Jesus. In chapter 23 Jesus has had a serious run-in with the religious leaders of His day and they are determined to kill Him[1]. In chapter 25 Yeshua's teaching moves on to set out the sober truth that parts of 'the church' will not be ready to receive Him when He returns in Glory (25: 1-13 and 25: 14-30). Sadly there will be many surprised faces amongst 'professing' Christians on the *Day of Judgment*. The most chilling words in the entire Bible (in your author's opinion) are those of Jesus in Matthew 7:23. In chapter 25 Jesus repeats a teaching on which He has been consistent – that some are self-deluded in their 'following' of the Lord. If in the Bible we are told clearly that not all Israel is Israel (Romans 9:6), should we be surprised, in a sense, that not all the church is in truth *the church*?

Matthew chapter 24 provides teaching that arises from the disciples' directing of Jesus' attention towards the grandeur of the Temple complex (24: 1). It seems that humanly-speaking they were mightily impressed with what was certainly one of the marvels of the ancient world. But Jesus can see beyond these human architectural statements of pride. He knows that the whole edifice will come tumbling down within one generation of His Own crucifixion[2]. Later (24:3) they ask Yeshua to explain Himself, as they specifically enquire what will be the sign of the end of *the age*. As we explored in chapter one of this book, down through history countless Christians have struggled with the "signs" that Yeshua gives and wondered, *is this the age in which I am living?*

As we suggested in chapter 4, Christians have tried to assemble their eschatological 'jigsaw picture' with one essential piece of the jigsaw missing (or ignored). That is, the position of Israel in God's end times purpose. Once Israel was reinstalled (in May 1948) in her ancient homeland, fully in accordance with biblical prophecy, so the proverbial 'clock' of world history passed midnight for the final time. The "signs" which Jesus gave should now fall into place with more clarity and greater immediacy. The institutional churches are likely to become ever more strident in their denunciation of Israel in their supposed 'concern' for what they call *the Palestinians*[3]. Whilst it is very legitimate to be concerned for the plight of Arab Israelis, the institutional

---

1 See David Serle and Peter Sammons **"Three Days and Three Nights that Changed the World"** for further insight into the final days of Jesus. The decision of the authorities to kill Jesus (we might say to judicially murder Jesus) was a long-standing one; it was not occasioned solely because of Jesus' denunciations of them in Matthew chapter 23.
2 The Temple was destroyed in AD70.
3 There has never been a country called Palestine – if readers dispute this, then answer this question, who was the first King of Palestine, and who was the last?

churches' obsession with this subject, and their often deafening silence on the subject of severely persecuted Christians in many countries of the world[4], leads one to the conclusion that there is a deep seated spiritual dynamic at work in this matter.

The day before these words were written, your author listened to the online recorded debates at the 2021 UK *Methodist Conference*, as its 'delegates' discussed a BDS resolution against Israel (carried, incidentally, by a considerable majority). One of the female speakers demanded that 'the soldiers of Hamas' should be referred to as 'soldiers', and not as terrorists! So much for the gentle sex![5] The condescension, moral outrage (against Israel but not her enemies) and over-arching detestation of Israel amongst modern Methodists (not all Methodists, in fairness, but a vast majority, especially in the West) stands in stark contrast to the attitude of Charles Wesley, the founder and great hymn writer of Methodism. Charles Wesley held a *Classical Zionist* understanding and his hymn "Almighty God of Love" expresses quite clearly that God's intention is to reveal His salvation purposes through Jews (verse 2), that all Israel will be saved (verses 3 and 4). Wesley saw that Jerusalem would "arise" again (verse 4) and that God would call the Hebrews home from East, West, North and South (verse 5). Finally that with Israel's myriads, all the nations would join with her as God's family would then be complete (verse 6). We have included Wesley's hymn in full as Appendix 7 to this book to confirm his clear understanding. What on earth would Charles Wesley make of modern Methodists?

The hatred by the institutional churches toward modern Israel is a subject that has been explored by many writers and we cannot, in this book, become too diverted into that particular subject area[6]. Author Peter Sammons devoted two chapters of his earlier book "Rebel Church" to exploring how a reconnection with the Hebraic root of the Christian faith is likely to be a facet of the End Time, as many Christians will "see" and understand (and rejoice in) God's covenantal faithfulness to His ancient Chosen People. The institutional churches will either love this and rejoice in it, or hate it and try to overturn it. Most, it seems, will hate it. We need say no more here but if readers want to access the book "Rebel Church", it is freely available online as a PDF[7].

---

4 Relatively few churches mark "Suffering Church Sunday" as a formal annual remembrance.
5 For a comment piece on this 2021 Methodist 'resolution', see
  https://christiancomment.org/?s=a+reason+to+hate
6 Recommended: "*Father Forgive Us – A Christian Response to the Church's Heritage of Jewish Persecution*" (Fred Wright, Monarch Publishing, 2002).
7 Chapters 7 and 8 are particularly relevant, and posit that the institutional churches' hatred of Israel is caused partly by an unholy envy of Israel, coupled to the realisation that the era of 'Church' dominance is drawing rapidly to a close. This is doubly troubling to those who hold to their 'theology' of Dominionism.

So one lesson for today is that Israel will not depart from the news channels of our world for long – there are too many and too diverse agendas aimed at undermining Israel. A second lesson is that the love of most will grow cold (Matthew 24:12). Here we are left wondering whether this is the 'love' of the world at large, or of the church, or both. Taken in conjunction with 24:13 it appears that the Lord is speaking principally of the professing 'church'. The huge and unprecedented rebellion of the institutional churches against the Holy Spirit that we increasingly encounter today, as every Biblical 'norm' is now openly challenged amongst and within those institutions, seems to be precisely what Jesus is referencing and anticipating in Matthew chapter 24.

Beyond church rebellion, yes, the love of most of those outside *The Kingdom* also will grow cold, which suggests that for all its 'woke' agendas, today's society will increasingly be marked by more and more violence and rivalry, not to mention violence against the unborn child (in 2021 the total number of abortions in the UK since abortion was legalised in 1997 stands in excess of nine millions – interestingly, approximately the same number that have migrated to the UK from other nations over the same period) and violence against the elderly and infirm as so-called 'mercy killings' become legalised[8].

Jesus gave us the sober warnings of Matthew Chapter 24 not to satisfy our idle curiosity, nor to shock, or to entertain. No, He gave us these sober warnings so that we can be prepared and recognise. Whilst the precise day and hour are unknown (though how that particular statement of Yeshua should be interpreted remains the subject of some discussion amongst Christians) we will know with increasing certainty precisely because Yeshua forewarned us and gave us clear 'clues' as to what to expect.

Deception

Before we leave Mathew 24 we should reflect for a moment that Yeshua warns specifically of deception. Our spiritual enemy the devil is out to deceive. The devil is a liar and the father of lies, says Jesus (John 8:44), so we should not be surprised that he seeks to spread confusion on this matter of the End Time. It seems likely that some of the "prophets" of previous eras who "prophesied" the imminent end of the world, even naming dates and times, were energized by the devil[9]. Why? So as to discredit eschatological anticipation and ensure that anyone who explores

---

8 See article "Kind Killers" in **Christian Comment** online magazine which looks at this question specifically https://christiancomment.org/2020/11/02/kind-killers/
9 A simple Google search on the Jehovas' Witnesses and their frequent prophecies of the end of the world will be instructive!

this subject will be considered to be a little bit 'wacky', and best avoided!

In Matthew 24: 4 Jesus warns that we should take care that we are not *deceived*. This suggests of course, both that it is possible to be deceived but also perfectly possible to avoid deception, especially as we are guided by the Holy Spirit. We know which 'camp' we should aim to be! Says Yeshua:

> "See to it that no one **deceives** you. For many will come in My name, claiming, 'I am the Christ', and will deceive many. You will hear of wars and rumours of wars, but see to it that you are not alarmed. These things must happen, but the end is still to come. Nation will rise against nation, and kingdom against kingdom. There will be famines and earthquakes in various places. All these are the beginning of birth pains" (Matthew 24:4-8).

The key deception is that of false Messiahs – and these have been a feature of the religious landscape, including Christianity, since the earliest times. War and natural disasters will also be a feature of *the end*, but we should recognise the prevalence of these things as the beginning, and imminence, of the end time.

> "At that time, if anyone says to you, 'Look, here is the Christ!' or 'There He is!' do not believe it. For false Christs and false prophets will appear and perform great signs and wonders that would **deceive** even the elect, if that were possible. See, I have told you in advance" (Matthew 24: 23-25).

Again we have Jesus' clear directive, some will masquerade as the Messiah (or "Christ") before Jesus returns, but we are not to believe them. They will be so convincing that, if it were possible to trick the Elect, then these evil deceivers would be able to do so. We should not be caught out, however, if we remain in Him. But many outside The Kingdom will indeed be deceived, and no doubt will persecute those who fail to follow or acknowledge their false Messiahs. Incidentally, some of history's terrible rulers have been seen as almost Messiah-like or divine figures. We have only to think of Adolf Hitler to see how religious-like fervour can be whipped-up and spread amongst the populace. At the time of writing in 2021 there was a Covid "jab" (or "vaccine") heavily promoted as a sort of scientific "messiah" and those who refused to take this medicine were considered almost as 'heretics' because of their refusal to *believe* in (and in some cases to *receive*) this saviour-like drug. In this there may be disturbing parallels with the ease with which whole populations can be energized and channeled with almost messianic zeal. As regards false Messiahs, Jesus could not be clearer: "do not believe it" (v. 26).

Deception, then, is something we must take seriously, but not be over-awed by. When deception comes it will be both subtle and emphatic at the same time. Our "secret weapon", however, is the Holy Spirit, Who will guide us into all truth. At this point readers may wish to go back and read Matthew Chapter 24 in its entirety. Sobering it may be, but the signals of which Jesus forewarns are ones for which we must be alert. Of course Matthew 24 is far from 'the be all and end all' of Biblical guidance on eschatology. It is, however, the Lord's Own summary of what to expect, and on that basis is worthy of double consideration by the true Berean Christian. Its counterpart is Luke Chapter 21 which recounts much of the same material as Matthew.

Luke reminds us that there will be huge fear amongst the world's general population and that "natural" phenomena will be signals that the end is at hand (Luke 21: 11). What Luke adds is the intriguing truth that "the time of the Gentiles" will have been "fulfilled" (Luke 21: 24). Many Bible-believing commentators understand this (and your author concurs) to reflect that fact that Israel will be in control of its own lands once again. Israel's recreation in May 1948 seems to be a clear signal that those "Gentile times" are now concluded. In turn, this may explain the subliminal (and demonic?) desire of so many of the world's nations to undermine Israel as a political and cultural reality – they believe that by so doing they can delay, or perhaps even divert entirely, God's stated purposes and Jesus' return. They are sorely mistaken . . .

CHAPTER 10

THE GOSPEL IN THE LAST DAYS
AND THE END TIME

**we have not received the spirit of the world but the Spirit
who is from God, that we may understand what God has freely given us
(1 Corinthians 2:12).**

So what is the Gospel?

It is strange, perhaps, that Christians can sometimes be "all at sixes and sevens"[1] in terms of precisely what is the gospel. One would think that this is, after all, the 'core product' of Christianity, and we so often speak of "the good news" and try to witness this good news to non-believers. Your author was once with a group of UK evangelists and asked the open question "so precisely what is the good news?", as he wanted to see how a group of 'professionals' would respond. This was surely not an 'unfair' question to spring upon them, but perhaps the fact that we were in a circular group with everyone listening (!) meant that some folk were more reticent than usual. No evangelist wants to look anything less than sure-footed in such a situation. There was a short uncomfortable silence and then one or two piped up with the stock answers of "well, it's the love of God" and "it's the good news that God will forgive you, eternally" and "it's the good news of eternal peace". Interestingly it was one of the non-professionals in the group who hit the proverbial nail 'bang on the head'. She said "it is the good news of the Kingdom".

The Bible is clear that Yeshua preached and taught the good news of the Kingdom: "*. . . he went throughout all Galilee, teaching in their synagogues and proclaiming the gospel of the Kingdom and healing every disease and every affliction among the people*" (Matthew 4:23). While Yeshua was physically on this Earth, He preached the good news of God's Kingdom, of *His* kingdom. Mark's gospel account says much the same: "*. . . after John was put in prison, Jesus came to Galilee, preaching the gospel of the kingdom of God, and saying, "The time is fulfilled, and the kingdom of God is at hand. Repent, and believe in the good news*." (Mark 1:14-15).

---

1 A Bristish colloquialism for being in a muddle!

Christians have long debated the 'what', 'when', 'where', and 'how' of the Kingdom of God. Some say that the Kingdom is yet to come, being still in the future, while others argue for something more abstract that takes place in the present. Your author thinks of *The Kingdom* as being principally *the saving rule and reign of God*. The Kingdom of God is all of those places where The Lord's will is taken seriously. This Kingdom is within us, as it presently resides in people's 'hearts' where God reigns. But one day God's rule will be manifest in this world[2], and it will not be universally comfortable!

There is a 'now' and a 'then' aspect to this; the Kingdom is indeed growing and global but it obviously does not hold sway in this present world. Jesus said to Pontius Pilate directly that His Kingdom is not of this world, because if it had been, then His disciples would have come and fought for it (John 18:36). So we know that although the Kingdom is inaugurated, it is not yet here in full force and effect. Yeshua taught His disciples to pray "**Your kingdom come, your will be done on earth as it is in heaven**" (Matthew 6:10-11), surely indicating that, although this Kingdom is on its way in, its triumph and fulfillment remain yet in the future, and our greatest desire *should* be to see it fully in effect in this world.

Jesus, by the way, never preached a gospel of love! Whilst love (or more correctly 'agape') is an aspect of and a symbol of the Kingdom, Jesus never said "the good news is that God loves you". No more did He say "the good news is that you can be forgiven eternally". Whilst both these are aspects of, and true out-workings of, the gospel, in and of themselves they are not THE gospel. No, the good news is that God's Kingdom is at hand and it is so close that we can reach out and grab hold of it. In Matthew 11:12, Jesus made the interesting statement that "**the Kingdom of God is forcefully advancing and forceful men lay hold of it**." No man (or woman) will be able to say they could not have reached out for the Kingdom had they really wanted to – it may not be easy to lay hold of, but it is certainly not out of reach!

What, then, does the Kingdom mean for us now? We must appreciate the metaphor of the ekklesia (or "church") as *an embassy* of the Kingdom: in 2 Corinthians 5: 20, Paul says that believers "**are ambassadors for Christ, God making his appeal through us**." This political language was very fitting during the time of Paul's writing. For Christians to proclaim "Jesus is Lord" was not merely a religious declaration but it was also unavoidably political. The Romans understood this as a rejection of their god-Emperor while the Jews understood it as a direct attack on their religious authorities. The ekklesia is a People who experience the rule of Messiah Yeshua collectively, as those *willingly submitted*

---

2 See our chapter 13.

to His Lordship above all else. We are a distinct 'People' as citizens of the Messiah's kingdom, having a unique mindset, worldview, ethic, and purpose in life. We are ambassadors for Messiah, inviting people into His glorious Kingdom and declaring that this eternal King has come to save the lost. We preach that one day He will return again to destroy the power of sin and establish an everlasting new heaven and new earth. Our words, then, should echo those of Jesus in saying, "**The time is fulfilled, and the kingdom of God has come near; repent and believe in the good news**" (Mark 1:15).

Readers who want to delve more deeply into the wonders of the Gospel may want to check-out the free resource "The Bible Student" and its study # 8 "The Gospel", which is freely available online as downloadable PDF[3]. Our question quite simply in this chapter is, how has the gospel been presented during the reality of the Last Days, as we defined these Last Days in Chapter 2? Remember that the last days are those from the time of the outpouring of the Holy Spirit at Pentecost, until Jesus returns.

Plainly the understanding from the earliest times of the Christian era was that this same era is "the last days" for Mankind. It was (and is) the last opportunity for peace with God on His terms – and remember, those are the only terms that are available! In these last days the urgency is to tell out the good news of Jesus, of His salvation via the cross and of our need to close with this offer of peace; we might add, this offer of *eternal* peace. The gospel in these last days has been marked by indifference, sneering and active persecution, waxing and waning in intensity and interspersed with periodic Kingdom revivals and outpourings. The spiritual battle, it seems, has see-sawed between the devil's apparent advantage and God's obvious advance through His wonderful Holy Spirit. During these last days the gospel has indeed advanced across planet Earth just as Yeshua commanded (Matthew 28: 19). We praise God for this, and today there is no place on planet Earth where the name of Yeshua (or variously Jesus, or Jesu, or Iesous) has not been encountered. Perhaps it is true to say that there are places in the world where the name of Jesus is scarcely known for a range of reasons, and perhaps God will yet 'turn up the volume' on missionary activity towards the end of these last days. But we can say that down through two millennia the Kingdom has been growing and advancing.

During these last days the gospel has been the number one concern of the ekklesia – at least in theory. Historically we can say that where the Church has foundered, generally it is because *the gospel* has been swamped by other agendas. When the gospel has been paramount, so the Kingdom has extended

---

3 At time of writing freely available here: https://christian-publications-int.com/images/PDF/ BibleStudent/08_GOSPEL.pdf There are some fifty free studies available on the CPI website.

and the ekklesia has grown. As a by-product, society has broadly improved – at least in the social sense[4].

Does the Gospel change in the End Time?

Does the gospel in any way change during the end time? Whilst emphases and even methods may change, the gospel itself is unchanging. Emphases on what is important and timely may indeed change. One example will suffice to illustrate this: in the Western world Christianity is no longer the dominant and accepted worldview. Accordingly we must learn to present gospel truth in a changed environment, where our modern Western world increasingly looks like the ancient Graeco-Roman world – a world of syncretism and religious pluralism, a world of moral relativism and social decay, where life is held cheap. In this changing environment *our* emphasis on the uniqueness of Messiah Yeshua and His achievement on the Cross must change, if only by becoming more prominent. By the same token methods may change as the old tried-and-tested appeal to the guilt-ridden sinner may have to adjust to the reality of a world where sin and rebellion are not only a daily reality, they are also actively celebrated, just as they were in Roman times. Finally it might be added that today there is an increasingly widespread belief that through science 'we' can engineer 'our' way out of any difficulty, thus faith is progressively being transferred to our modern 'scientists'.

How, then, might the gospel change in the end times and does the Bible itself speak of this? When Yeshua revealed aspects of the future in Matthew chapter 24 His teaching seems to move between the Last Days and the End Times as we have defined both. So in Matthew 24: 10-14 the emphasis seems to shift towards the end, where previously the Lord has been speaking of the ongoing and unceasing opposition of the world to the Gospel during the Pentecost era. From verse 15 onwards we can say with assurance that Jesus is speaking of the End, although it can be argued that His words would have been understood in the first century AD as foretelling the desecration of Jerusalem and its Temple by the Roman legions in AD70. There seems to be clear dual aspect in this that *we* can perceive given the benefit of hindsight. Many bible prophecies have both a near term and a far term outworking; Yeshua's discourse in Matthew 24 is in keeping with this biblical pattern.

---

4 See for example the secular book "Suicide of The West" by Richard Koch and Chris Smith, which openly acknowledges the impact of Christianity on social and technological progress through the past 1000 years, without which, the authors state, the West as we know it would never have existed. Neither would democracy have taken root. They believe that the de-Christiansation of the West will not adversely impact its democratic credentials. Your author is not so sanguine!

The times of the Gentiles

It is in the Gospel of Luke that Yeshua refers to the conclusion of *the times of the Gentiles*. In Luke 21: 24 Jesus uses this specific phrase. Our very first question is 'what is the context'? Straightway we must observe that Luke 21[5] is the same discourse as Mathew 24, but Luke through his own interviews and investigations (see Luke 1: 1-4, but particularly verse 3) has picked up a detail that Matthew omitted. Jesus says: **Let those who are in Judea flee to the mountains, and let those who are inside the city depart, and let not those who are out in the country enter it, for these are days of vengeance, to fulfill all that is written. Alas for women who are pregnant and for those who are nursing infants in those days! For there will be great distress upon the earth and wrath against this people. They will fall by the edge of the sword and be led captive among all nations, and Jerusalem will be trampled underfoot by the Gentiles, until the times of the Gentiles are fulfilled** (Luke 21: 21-24).

A natural reading of these words and the context leads us to the obvious conclusion that the Lord is prophesying and referencing the sacking of Jerusalem by the Legions in AD70, and the subsequent deportations of Jews to the four corners of the Roman Empire, which in turn would lead to a Jewish diaspora of global proportions. Even today there are more Jewish people outside Israel than within. So far, so straightforward! But what does the fulfillment of *the times of the Gentiles* actually mean? This is where controversy creeps in.

A straightforward contextual approach to this indicates that, whilst Israel will be exiled, eventually she will return and the lands that hitherto have been under Gentile domination will revert to Jewish control (and we might add, naturally, that physical Israel would again arise as a political reality). Not only is this a natural reading of what is said, it also chimes-in with the broader question of Israel in the New Testament. (Bible teacher David Pawson has explored the whole question of Israel in the New Testament context, and there is nothing we wish to add here. Readers are directed to his "Israel in the New Testament" – where Pawson treats this subject exhaustively in 220 pages). This understanding, incidentally, has been the clear insight of many

---

5 We are of course aware that some commentators, with good reason, posit that Luke chapter 21 may also have a dual realisation, or a double fulfilment. To Luke's first readers, Luke 21 would probably have been seen as fulfilled in AD70. Yet some modern commentators think that there may also be a future repetition where Israel may again be invaded and (temporarily) defeated pursuant to the false peace engineered by the Antichrist. Your author acknowledges the reality of the argument and the grounds on which it is based, but at this point he does not have a definitive view or 'position' on this. As we have said elsewhere, we presently 'peer as through a glass, darkly'...

bible teachers over hundreds of years and is sometimes called a "Classical Zionism" hermeneutic. There are other 'theologians', however, who resist this idea and argue, implausibly we believe, that once Jewish people were exiled by Rome so all of God's purposes were 'fulfilled', and the times of the Gentiles is *the Christian era* until Messiah Jesus returns. This idea is driven by their over-arching hermeneutic called "Replacement Theology" (otherwise called "Fulfillment Theology") which perceives Israel and the Jews as having no special role in God's ongoing purposes.

We will not argue the point further here. So many good and serious writers and teachers have explored this matter so thoroughly in preceding generations that we could only repeat what others have already said. Rather we will make the simple comment, that Jesus was clear that Israel would fulfill a special role at the end, and this role would be inaugurated in some way by the evident conclusion of *the times of the Gentiles*. Your author concurs with so many others that the time of "trampling" by the Gentiles upon Israel ended in May 1948 when Israel again became a nation-state[6]. Attempts to argue differently seem to be energised by a clear agenda of supercessionism ('replacement/fulfillment' theology), and to be in-credible when compared with what the Lord Himself said, and what Scripture otherwise reveals.

Some 'conservative' Christians interpret the Scriptures through a 'Replacement' prism. Whilst these may hold a high view of Scripture, their a-priori agenda is that Israel has no place in God's plans. So Luke 21:24 is "spiritualised" into a "spiritual kingdom" which is in normative opposition to God and thus characterised as "the times of the Gentiles" following which Messiah Jesus returns and "the church militant" becomes the church triumphant – associated with the return of Messiah Jesus physically to this Earth[7]. Liberal theologians and clerics, by contrast, who hold a low-view of Scripture, argue that Luke 21:24 is meaningless (or mysterious or false) and should not be a focal point in Christian understanding. Theologians *on both extremes* are rather on the back-foot, we believe, as a simple natural reading of what Jesus says is decidedly that non-Jews (i.e. Gentiles) will control Israel until God determines to put His ancient People back in their Promised Land. We repeat that in May 1948 the times of the Gentiles concluded, which suggests that *from that date* the world is approaching its End in this present era. Furthermore, in this sense, many would say that we can now distinctly "hear"

---

6 Some argue that the times of the Gentiles ended in 1967 when Jerusalem came again under Israeli control. This idea has merit and the truth may be that the period 1948-67 is the time during which a new era was ushered-in, and 'the times of the Gentiles' ended.

7 This theological construct is sometimes referred to as "Dominionism", or "Dominion Theology"; and also variously as "Kingdom Now", "Latter Rain" and "Postmillennialism".

Jesus' footfall approaching. We would expect prophetic signs to reinforce this. They seem to be!

Does the gospel itself change, then, during the End Times? We would tentatively say 'yes', in the sense that the nearness of Jesus' return (be it mere generations away or yet hundreds of years) will become an integral part of the Good News message. As this world continues its slide into God-opposed anarchy, so there will be increasing general societal anguish at the disasters yet to materialise.

Scripture speaks of a time of "tribulation" (or *big troubles* – refer to Daniel chapter 9 – and see in particular our next chapter, in *this* book). The message of the gospel has been, in any case, rather 'individualised' as Christians in the West have spoken so much of the need for personal commitment, personal baptism, and personal rebirth. In recent decades, however, this seems to have become a parody of the true gospel, and has almost come to be seen as a lifestyle choice based on "individualism". Self-actualisation or 'individualism' is a Western concept and resonates far less in the collective consciousness of the non-OECD world, and indeed the non-democratic world. In other parts of the world, the *corporate* (group) implications of the gospel may loom larger in people's thinking. The Western world is arguably dying-out (through huge abortion matched by equally huge inwards migration from non-western societies, through the reality of "spermageddon"[8] and through conscious decisions to delay child-bearing until relatively late in life with the concomitant determination to procreate at less than true "replacement" rates – which historically has been considered as 2.4 children per family). The 'growing' or 'burgeoning' non-OECD world may perceive the gospel and the Kingdom differently and, dare we say it, more correctly?

We believe that the *true gospel* message will increasingly be seen as the definitive "answer" to Mankind's collective problems, but only as it *links* the over-arching personal need for personal Salvation with the evident reality of progressive social decay (Acts 2: 40 "**Save yourself from this corrupt generation**"). This social unraveling will lead to rebellion, lawlessness and warfare. The world's (and the institutional Churches') intolerance of Israel both as a nation-state and as a religious expression will be a feature of this End Time reality. A buddy of author Peter Sammons states, from time to time, that Mankind is "too stupid" to survive and that consequently our days are numbered (he has Roman Catholic leanings). There may be a grain of truth in what he says, at least in the sense that Scripture is clear that "**the fool has said in his heart that there**

---

8 Decline in male fertility

is no God" (Psalm 14: 1). Today's God-denying society is a society for which its collective future contains huge (existential?) storm clouds.

But our buddy is perhaps missing something more obvious. It is not so much stupidity and sinfulness (rebellion against God's right to rule – and rebellion therefore against the Kingdom) that are Mankind's ultimate undoing. The Bible is clear that Mankind collectively – and in large part – will not repent at the End, and so will not turn back to their Creator God for Salvation and safety. The book of Revelation indicates continued and determined rebellion right up until the return of Messiah Jesus. Surely that sort of rebellion is indeed stupid, when Mankind has been given so many chances *and Jesus has already paid on the Cross the ultimate price of all Mankind's rebellion*. To ignore so great a salvation is indeed "stupid" as much as it is anything else! But the good news remains that until the very End, still a remnant will continue to turn to Him and so to be Saved! Praise God for that wonderful truth.

Troublingly, the institutional churches' perspective on the good news (gospel) seems today to be leading inexorably towards "a different gospel" (Galatians 1: 6-8). In our schematic below we simply acknowledge that from the First Century AD (in fact, during these Last Days as we have defined that term in this book, from the time of Pentecost) the institutional churches' approach to the good news has "evolved" or "developed", arguably placing increasing distance between what is taught and practised to what Jesus actually revealed. In the first century, the gospel was totally "christo-centric" (Jesus focused) and to "own" His Name then was potentially to court disaster, as it is still today in, for example, Iran or North Korea. Yet the inevitable exclusivism in being called into a family, as an *elect in Christ*, moved progressively to "church-ism" where salvation was sought in structures and traditions. In church-ism the priest became 'king'. From this the church moved more towards pluralism as it encountered inevitable 'philosophical' questions around the world's dizzying array of belief systems. It was a relatively short 'hop' from there to 'godism' where the only *constant* became the belief in a 'god' who was pretty much obliged to 'save all', irrespective. And from godism we seem today to be very close to the emergence of a new world religion, possibly to be headed eventually by that person known in Scripture as the "Antichrist". Our schematic below captures these ideas.

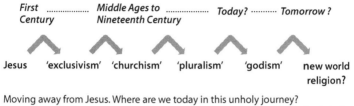

Salvation – the institutional church's changing perspective

First .... Middle Ages to .... Today? .... Tomorrow ?
Century   Nineteenth Century

Jesus   'exclusivism'   'churchism'   'pluralism'   'godism'   new world
                                                                 religion?

Moving away from Jesus. Where are we today in this unholy journey?
How can we find our way back to Jesus and are the institutional 'churches' a help,
or a hindrance?

These uncomfortable questions are increasingly encountered by Christians.

How do we respond? How to we define 'Christian'?

LED 18

We acknowledge that the above is a simplification. The *body of believers* was assailed by heretical forces almost from day one, and the first century was not necessarily a golden age of Christianity. Even so, the trajectory of de-Christianisation is arguably well enough captured in the illustration. Your author foresees, then, a 'sharpening' of the gospel message that will intelligently – and astutely – link the realities of world events in the End Time to the need for personal Salvation – indeed to the need for *re-birth* in the emphatic words of Yeshua (John 3:3 and 7). This 'sharpening' will not involve idle speculation on times and specific dates, but it certainly will more clearly recognise 'where we are at' in terms of God's supreme purpose. We certainly anticipate that more false teachers will emerge who will try to predict times and dates, but they will be shown up for what they are. They will succeed, however, in bringing eschatological teaching into disrepute, and that is sad. We conclude, then, that in these senses the Gospel message does indeed change or amend in the End Time.

CHAPTER 11

DANIEL'S SEVENTY WEEKS

**there is a judge for the one who rejects me and does not
accept my words; the very words I have spoken
will condemn them at the last day (John 12:48).**

End Time Confusion?

It is remarkable the extent to which both Old and New Testament Scriptures reveal aspects of the End Times. God has been telling His people about the end - from almost the beginning! Christians have attempted for two millennia to acquire some precision in understanding how we are to recognise the end, how to prepare for it, and to what extent (and how) to preach about it. On the latter two aspects, the institutional church[1] has done rather badly, with mixed messages and frankly wrong interpretations. Its principal achievement, perhaps, has been to bring exegesis of the End Time into broad disrepute. This is a tragedy, given that God has graciously given His people clear signposts of what to look out for. The proactive activity of the enemy in sowing end times confusion is not to be discounted.

As we have seen, the Lord Jesus spoke distinctly about the end and posed the question: **"when the Son of Man comes, will he find faith on the earth?"** The overall sense of Scripture is that indeed the Lord will not find (much) faith on the earth, and that Mankind's rebellion will continue unabated and un-repented until the very end. Most serious Bible expositors highlight four prophetic books and the Gospels themselves as setting out the key contours of the End Time events. As we saw earlier, Jesus spoke clearly and unambiguously about the end time and this is recorded for us generally in Matthew chapter 24 and its equivalent, Luke chapter 21. Amongst the key prophets, the book of Revelation is unique in the New Testament as being its only fully prophetic, forward looking, book. In the Old Testament, Ezekiel, Daniel and Zechariah reveal aspects of the end for Mankind[2]. The exegete's challenge has always

---

1 not to mention some decidedly dodgy latter day 'prophets'
2 Arguably aspects of end time prophecy are scattered right across the Tanach ('Old Testament'). Isaiah chapters 24-26 fall into this category.

been to understand (and ideally to 'map') the interrelated narrative that opens up to the diligent Bible searcher. It is not a straightforward task . . .

In appendices 1 to 4 we have attempted to draw out the key themes and currents that the Bible opens up and to invite readers to make their own assessment as to what extent these themes are reflective of today's international realities. The fact that Yeshua Himself told His disciples to 'look out' (Matthew 24: 4; Luke 21: 8) indicates this is not merely an intellectual exercise, or even a test of faith. It is far more practical than that: we are to be alert, aware and even *on the qui-vivre* for what Jesus warned. It is vitally important to our own spiritual health and wellbeing, and this was not some helpful suggestion from our Lord Jesus – it was a distinct command. We might add, it is also a sign of intelligence and basic maturity for a Believer to display some degree of interest in the future. It helps us to live out our today, and to withstand the pressures of tomorrow. Our task, then, is to attempt to 'follow' the revealing of the future through Ezekiel, Daniel and Zechariah and to map these across to the book of Revelation. Plainly this is not idle curiosity, nor an opportunity to demonstrate 'cleverness' or Biblical astuteness. Rather, it is an attempt to help prepare for a future that may lie not too far ahead . . .

The very first thing to say is that the future is mapped out in the code language of Babylon. So, in Revelation at the end of the Bible, it is 'Babylon' that finally falls. Christians understand 'Babylon' variously as nations, regions and/ or politico-economic systems. Some see Babylon as principally the ex-Christian West. Others see Babylon as incorporating all the global power blocs – and in this day and age that would naturally include China. Still others see Babylon as the world's intellectual, power, finance, trading and religious *systems* all bound up together. There are arguments for each of these positions and each position can provide a helpful perspective.

'Babylon' is, in the Bible, symbolic of the World's power structures that stand against God's faithful people. As God's Name and reputation is always associated with His *Chosen People* Israel, we see a simple historical truth that the ancient Babylonian empire would be used to effect God's "judgment" on His rebellious nation Israel. Earlier in this book, in chapter 8, we briefly considered the ancient Babylonian exile events, and how the key prophets interpreted the signs of their own times. Our task today is not dissimilar . . .

What we can say right now is that the key Bible books of Ezekiel, Daniel, Zechariah and Revelation are intimately interconnected and concern the spiritual and physical (socio-political) reality of Babylon – which is, collectively, all of the World's systems *still* directed against God's faithful people. Rather beyond the scope of this book, but noteworthy, is that 'God's people' today comprise men and women from every tribe and tongue who are 'called' into His Kingdom and rejoice together as those *saved by grace* under the 'new covenant' of Grace. It would take a whole book to adequately explore these truths so we will not try to 'defend' any of our assertions now. It is author Alex Jacob who points out, helpfully, that the relationship of the "old" Abraham-Moses covenant with the "new" covenant of Grace, is one of "enlargement" of those older covenant promises so as to encapsulate all who place their trust and faith in Yeshua ha Massiasch (Jesus the Messiah[3]).

In projecting the contours of the End Times, what do Ezekiel, Daniel, and Zechariah add to the 'picture'?

Three prophets, three exiles, three returns

As we saw in chapter 8, these key prophets compass a 'big story'. Each projects forward into our future as well as prophesying about events unfolding in the lives of their own generation. Ezekiel's big theme was impending judgment, yet he 'saw' a glorious and peaceful future – a future that plainly has not yet arrived! God referred to Ezekiel as "**son of man**" (Ezekiel 3:17) who was a watchman over Israel. Jesus of course is the eternal Son of Man and saw Himself in the same way (e.g. Mark 10: 45), although we might add that Yeshua clearly sees Himself as a watchman over a greater and enlarged Israel – a spiritual Israel (see Alex Jacob, *The Case for Enlargement Theology*, for a full exploration of this subject). In Ezekiel, God is crystal clear that desolation awaits because of Israel's serial rebellions: "**I am about to bring a sword against you, and I will destroy your high places. Your altars will be desolated and your shrines smashed**" (Ezekiel 6: 3-4). Yet her "**survivors will remember me among the nations where they are taken captive**". Wherever Israel has been exiled throughout history, her people have 'remembered' their God – the God of Abraham and of Isaac and of Jacob (for example, see the Bible's book of *Lamentations*).

It is in **Ezekiel** chapter 13 that the 'son of man' is instructed to speak against the prophets of Israel, who had brought false messages. We are left today with those memorable and searing words: "**they have led my people astray, saying "Peace" when there is no peace, and since when a flimsy wall is being built they plaster it with whitewash. Therefore tell those who are**

---

3 Note in particular Alex Jacob's leading treatise: "The Case For Enlargement Theology", which charts a helpful practical course between the twin errors of Replacement (or 'fulfilment') Theology, and Two Covenant Theology. Author Peter Sammons increasingly thinks of these two false theologies as the twin "ugly sisters" of Christian teaching!

plastering it, it will fall". Yes, their wall of pride and self-reliance certainly did fall. We are left wondering to what extent, today, we can apply Ezekiel's words to our own church leaders (and flocks) who preach *another gospel* (Galatians 1: 8; 2 Corinthians 11: 4) which does not depend upon the finished work of Jesus, but rather on some 'religion of love', where anything goes. Are these today's false prophets? Will their world similarly come crashing down?

In Ezekiel chapters 40 to 48 the prophecies switch focus to an eternal reckoning. In chapter 40 Ezekiel is 'taken' or 'transported' via visions (reminiscent of John's visions in Revelation) to a new and perfect Temple, in a new and perfect City. Plainly the language is highly symbolic, but the picture is clear; God's people will one day be "taken" to a place of perfection. And since today we live in a hugely imperfect world, we can conclude with assurance that this perfect City remains as yet in our future. This perfect City has a name - "**The Lord is There**" (Ezekiel 48: 35). Christians have long understood that our eternal future will be in that place where the Lord Himself is, when He 'tabernacles' amongst His people. And in Revelation we encounter a perfect City that has no Temple. Why? Because it is not necessary! The Lord Himself is there amongst His people, so we will need no Temple in which to worship Him. Praise God!

Our second prophet is **Daniel**. The book of Daniel is a combination of some of the best-known stories in the Bible (think – Daniel in the Lion's den; Shadrach, Meshach and Abednego in the fiery furnace; and Belshazzar's feast complete with "the writing on the wall"). Daniel's narrative is both hard to comprehend and highly symbolic. King Nebuchadnezzar's dream in chapter 2 is arguably a foresight of four separate empires – the Babylonian, the Medo-Persian, the Greek and the Roman. This reminds us that in spite of the 'greatness' of these man-made empires, God is firmly in control and knows the end from the beginning. Whilst these empires appear to be historical, there is a sense in which the Roman Empire lives on today in the shape of the Western World and the triumph of Greek philosophy in our modern world – reaching arguably as far afield as China – which today appears in some senses to be joining, philosophically, the Western world (although China would never admit it!).

In chapter 2 and verse 27 Daniel is clear that King Nebuchadnezzar is seeing a vision of the 'last days'. Now this vision certainly remains in our future as the key events have not yet transpired, as we shall see shortly, but we might also observe that parts of Daniel's meta-narrative certainly do lie in 'the last days' as we have understood and defined that term in this book – in other words in the Pentecost or 'Church' era of Grace. Yet Daniel also alludes directly to "the time of the end" (11: 40), so we can have absolute confidence that Daniel's prophecies are relevant to us today, and remain as yet a part of *our* future, too. King Nebuchadnezzar's prophetic dream in chapter 4 is given a full and proper interpretation by Daniel, but the practical working outcome seems to emphasise the key message of the Bible to all Mankind: "**Separate yourself from your sins by doing what is right, and from your injustices by showing mercy to the needy**" (4:27). This is an echo, surely, of the practical implications of following Jesus as Lord and as Saviour . . .

Daniel 'sees' two visitations of Messiah (7:13-14 and 10:5) but fails to understand them *as two* visitations. One 'like a son of man' comes who is "**given dominion and glory and a kingdom, so that those of every people, nation and language should serve him. His dominion is an everlasting dominion that will not pass away, and his kingdom is one that will not be destroyed**" (7:14). Christians understand this to be Yeshua, whose Kingdom was inaugurated at His first coming, a Kingdom that cannot now be overthrown despite the worst that "Babylon" can throw at it. What Daniel sees across the book that bears his name is in fact two different epochs – the first epoch covering the time up to Yeshua's first incarnation and the second being events leading up to His second coming. As David Pawson says in his "Unlocking the Bible", "*it is as if Daniel looked through a prophetic telescope and saw two 'peaks' of history, a lower in front of a higher, without realising the length of the valley between them*" (op cit page 649)). Daniel's "big picture" shows that a coming King will supersede all the kingdoms of the world.

Daniel's prophecy includes the raising up of one who opposes the son of man – described in Daniel's vision as "the little horn" (8: 9). Christians understand this as being the Antichrist. Daniel is told specifically that this part of his vision relates to the "time of the end" (8: 17 and 19). However, having been given a clear glimpse, Daniel is told that he is to "**seal up the vision because it refers to many days in the future**" (8: 26). Later in the book, we are told about a battle between kings of the south and the north which will be "at the time of the end" (11: 40). But once again, Daniel is told emphatically that what he has been given is "**secret and sealed until the time of the end**" (12: 9).

Whilst Christians have down through nineteen centuries rightly sought to understand these things, at least in outline, most have accepted that we must wait patiently for the full outworking. In addition we should not be overly dogmatic about prophetic details because at this time we simply do not know. In the future it is understood that *the signals* will get both clearer and stronger, and that there will be a palpable sense of the Lord's imminent return. We note that there have been many false 'prophecies' about the Lord's *imminent* return – think for example of the Jehovah's Witnesses who 'foretold' the second coming as happening in 1878, 1881, 1914, 1918, 1925 and 1975. Each time the so-called "Watchtower" was compelled to 'reinterpret' what actually happened – or rather, what didn't happen! They said these failures were other 'types' or 'signposts' to God's activity[4]. The 'JWs' are not alone in this abject failure of 'prophecy', but they certainly stand out as symbolic of a dreadful malaise and a hugely unhealthy interest in "the End". We must avoid falling into the same vice!

Irrespective of what we have just said, we note that Daniel's vision does help us to appreciate that there are *two* incarnations of the Son of Man, and that Yeshua's Kingdom, having been received by the Saints, will possess it **"forever and ever"** (7: 18). There will be a seeming triumph of the Antichrist (7: 21-22 and 23-26), but his time of success will be short-lived. Finally we should note that Yeshua Himself cited Daniel as being a reliable witness of whom we should be aware and take note – see Matthew 24: 15.

Our third prophet is **Zechariah**. He also understood Israel's troubles with their Babylonian captors as being judgmental both in cause and effect. In his first eight chapters Zechariah brings messages of warning, yet also of hope. Briefly in chapter 9 he alludes to judgment on Israel's neighbours. From chapters 9 to 14 he foresees a future of prosperity and peace. Thinking from our perspective in *this* book, we focus on chapters 12 to 14. Throughout Zechariah the repetitive phrase **"in those days"** is used. It begins when God states plainly that He will return to Zion (8: 3) and thereafter wherever we see the term "in those days" or **"on that day"** he is referring to this future time. In chapters 12 to 14, however, usage of the term goes into overdrive with some fifteen direct allusions to this prophetic future time.

Religious Jews as well as Christians understand chapters 12 to 14 as referencing a future that has not yet arrived. In this future it seems that somehow internationally Israel shall be at the heart or epicentre of developments, and Jerusalem itself will be an international focal point. In broad brushstrokes we can say that an international force will attack Israel (12: 1-9) and that pursuant to this a majority of Jews will recognise Messiah (12: 10). **"Then I will pour out a spirit of grace and prayer on the house of David and the residents of Jerusalem, and they will look at me whom they pierced. They will mourn for him as one mourns for an only child and weep bitterly for him as one weeps for a firstborn".** Christians understand this as a reflection and prefigured confirmation of Paul's later assertion that one day **"all Israel will be saved"** (Romans 11: 26).

So, three prophets! There were effectively three exiles via Babylon, as we saw in chapter 8. Yet there are *another three exiles* if we assume for a moment

---

4 https://en.wikipedia.org/wiki/Unfulfilled_Watch_Tower_Society_predictions, makes for rather unedifying reading on the antics of the Watchtower.

that the Babylonian exile was in reality a single event. It must be true that prophetically Ezekiel, Daniel and Zechariah are also reflecting a broader spiritual truth that rebellion (egregious sins) by God's people, whether Jewish or Christian, ultimately leads to disaster, loss and "exile" – even to the point of losing faith. So Israel's first exile was to Assyria in 722 BC. The second was to Babylon in 587 BC. The third was via Rome from AD 70 onwards. This third exile was the longest and bitterest, in the sense that Israel was excluded from her homeland for nigh-on 2,000 years and suffered hugely at the hands of so many oppressors, with an evil climax in the Nazi Holocaust (Shoah) which was Hitler's 'final solution' to what he saw as his 'Jewish problem'.

Our three prophets (as indeed other biblical prophets) see an ongoing role for Israel, and we note that God's promise to Abraham as the "father" of Israel was specifically to make him into a mighty nation that cannot be numbered (Genesis 12: 2 and 18: 18. See also Genesis 28: 14). As the Jewish diaspora today remains relatively small, Christians understand this mighty nation to incorporate all those who place their trust in the Jewish Messiah, who are thereby adopted into an *enlarged* nation – and indeed a *global* nation. Yet it is in Zechariah that we see most clearly Israel at the epicentre of End Time events. In 12: 2 Zechariah tells us that God "**will make Jerusalem a cup that causes staggering for the peoples who surround the city**". Various interpretations might help to open this out, but the meaning in our own day may partly reflect the fact that the nations that surround Israel have sought persistently to destroy her, and yet they only seem to bring God's judgment back upon themselves. The Middle East today remains a cauldron of uncertainty, insecurity and hopelessness – is this straightforwardly because they have chosen to try to destroy Israel?

Zechariah tells us that "**on that day [God] will make Jerusalem a heavy stone for all the peoples; all who try to lift it will injure themselves severely when all the nations of the world gather against her**" (12: 3). How sad, indeed! Surely this lies in the future as, thus far, the nations have not in a totally united sense risen up against Israel. We must conclude therefore that the final outworking of this prophecy remains in the future. And yet . . . Today we live in an era when the World believes that it has a 'Jewish problem' to which it seeks an agreed 'final solution', and that Jerusalem needs to have a 'final status' that will involve her sub-division into smaller cantons. Might not this final-status 'solution' essentially involve squeezing the Jewish community into smaller purely Jewish or Israeli areas? And if so, would it be unfair to refer to these smaller Jewish areas as 'ghettos'? Today, the United Nations has issued more censure resolutions against Israel than against any other single nation. At the time of writing it is difficult to be fully accurate as to numbers of censure motions, but adding all the UN 'agencies' together we find that since 1948 something in excess of fifty percent are directed solely at tiny Israel[5].

Three returns? Each exile/dispersion of Israel was followed by slow returns[6]. Many Christians have long understood as they looked at Bible prophecy that one day the nation of Israel would again become a reality, and that in some sense this would be associated with the return of Messiah Jesus – His second coming. The return of the global Jewish diaspora to Eretz Israel has for many been seen in this light. A basic question for all Christians is: "*is modern Israel a mistake, or is she part of God's unfolding plan*"? Plainly this is a key question and a notable 'point of departure' and controversy amongst Christians, as some say 'yes' and others 'no'.

As a 'snapshot' of the three Old Testament prophetic books and their single New Testament counterpart, our schematic on page 97 may be helpful. It is in the book of Revelation in the New Testament that we get our clearest sense of the *final battle* or "Armageddon" which humankind conspires to bring upon itself. Revelation tells us of the final downfall and destruction of Babylon. This seems to be a symbolic Babylon rather than a reconstituted city or political power, although we note that Iraq's late dictator Saddam Hussein had a dream to rebuild Babylon, so who knows? Perhaps one day someone will try this as well. The concept of 'Babylon' as a world system seems, however, to your author to be the more likely and most helpful explanation[7]. Revelation tells us of a final judgment and a new heaven and new earth (chapters 20 and 21 in total). Sadly the details of what all this means has been the cause of considerable controversy, upset, argument and schism amongst 'Christians', albeit the broad outline is recognised by most.

Daniel's Seventy Weeks

In the outline above Daniel's overall prophecy may seem relatively straightforward to grasp, at least in its broad brush-strokes. Yet in chapter nine Daniel's vision moves towards a very specific prophecy which is frankly difficult to get to grips with. People who do not want to acknowledge the prophetic accuracy of the Bible argue that certain parts of Daniel must have been written

---

5 A useful analytical resource, but we cannot vouch for its accuracy: https://en.wikipedia.org/wiki/List_of_United_Nations_resolutions_concerning_Israel. A second helpful resource is "UN Watch", cited here: https://unwatch.org/un-israel-key-statistics/
6 We acknowledge that the 'return' from Assyria never occurred in a decisive concrete form and so some speak of 'the ten lost tribes' of Israel. Yet inevitably a few Jewish people would have returned.
7 See David Lambourn – "Babel Versus Bible: The Battle for the Heart of Mankind", 2021, for a full exploration of this subject.

post-facto, as his prophecies have proved to be so accurate. Daniel chapter 8 described future developments corresponding to the rise of Alexander the Great, the division of Alexander's empire into four rival kingdoms, and the activity of Antiochus Epiphanes – a Syrian king who became a notorious enemy of Israel during the decade of 160BC.

Likewise Daniel chapter 11 contains information about unnamed national movements that are now history – the defeat of Medo-Persia by Greece, the partitioning of the Macedonian kingdom into four realms (11: 1-4), the wars between the Ptolemies and Seleucids (11: 5-20) and the great persecution under Antiochus Epiphanes (11: 21-35). These events are detailed with such vigour and clarity and match so precisely actual events in the fourth > third > second centuries BC, that atheists are compelled to claim these are later accretions to the basic text. Such atheists are on the back foot, however, as both textual criticism and the sheer existence of the Bible itself bear powerful witness to the veracity of the original record. The discovery of the Dead Sea Scrolls in 1948 also hugely undermined attempts to 'late-date' the Scriptures, as most serious scholars readily accept the affirmative value of these very early texts. With these thoughts in mind, we can turn our attention to Daniel chapter 9 and in particular to verses 20-27.

Whilst most of Daniel's prophecies were fulfilled before 150BC and were related to what we might call secular history, some are clearly Messianic. He recalls a vision in which he saw the "Ancient of Days" seated in the presence of the **"ten thousand times ten thousand"** (7: 9-10). He also saw **"One like the Son of Man, coming with the clouds of heaven"** to whom the Ancient of Days gave **"dominion and glory and a Kingdom . . . an everlasting dominion which shall not pass away"** (7: 13-14). So what about chapter 9 and *the seventy weeks*? Is this Messianic, too?

The place is Babylon, the year 538 BC and Daniel is now eighty years old. He has been reading the book of Jeremiah, which foretold the Babylonian exile, and now understands that God has decreed that Israel's time of captivity will be seventy years (Jeremiah 25: 11-12; 29: 10). This insight has deeply impressed Daniel, who longs to see Israel's return to her promised land. (As Daniel was himself captured in 605 BC, we calculate that some 67 years had now passed). But Daniel is unsure whether the "starting point" for the prophecy was 605 BC. He knows, for example, that the final Babylonian devastation of Jerusalem did not occur until 586 BC. Troubled by these uncertainties, Daniel begins to pray – he needs answers! In his prophetic book, Daniel shows to his own generation, and to succeeding generations, God's purposes. There was a bigger picture to be revealed.

In response to his prayers the angel Gabriel brought to Daniel a message that encompassed more than "just" the seventy years Daniel was exploring. What was brought seemed to be the "master timetable" of God's future Messianic scheme. The prophecy began by predicting that the messianic age would arrive after "seventy weeks". The majority of serious Bible exegetes, whether Jewish or Christian, interpret this to be seventy weeks of years – in other words 490 years. Some assume this to be literal, whilst others (who note that 7 and 70 often have symbolic significance) assume it to be a long and indeterminate time.

During these seventy weeks, rebellion (or transgression) will finish and there will be a stop to sin and *atonement* provided for iniquity (9: 24). With the word 'atonement', Christians naturally sit up and listen! Righteousness will be established that will also "seal up" all further vision and prophecy – in other words bring both vision and prophecy to an end. By this time the entire world will comprehend all past prophecies from the earliest of times and see that God has brought them all to pass, precisely as He has also blessed all Mankind. Finally, *the most holy One* will be anointed (9: 25). Some Jews and Christians see this as a rebuilding of the Jerusalem Temple. Overall your author does not find this view compelling; in common with the majority of exegetes, he understands this as being the anointing of Yeshua.

What most do agree upon is that, during this 'seventy week' programme, the world will see the end of spiritual rebellion, sin will be restrained, reconciliation accomplished, righteousness prevail and prophecy come to an end. And then God will finally either anoint a new Temple (minority view) or His Messiah (majority view). We now need to consider the 490 year timeline that Daniel predicts.

> Know and understand this:
> From the issuing of the decree
> to restore and rebuild Jerusalem
> until **an Anointed One**, the ruler,
> will be seven weeks and sixty-two weeks.
> It will be rebuilt with a plaza and a moat,
> but in difficult times.
> After those sixty-two weeks
> **the Anointed One** will be cut off
> and will have nothing.
> The people of the coming ruler
> will destroy the city and the sanctuary.
> The end will come with a flood,
> and until the end there will be war;
> desolations are decreed.   (Daniel 9: 25-26, CSB)

These verses cover sixty-nine of the seventy weeks of God's announced programme for Daniel's people and their city. The time period commences with 'the issuing of the decree to restore and rebuild Jerusalem', which seems to cite a definite official decree or authorisation to rebuild Jerusalem. If we can identify this decree then we know when the seventy weeks began.

The Bible recounts the issuing of three decrees authorising the Jews to return to their homeland. The first was by Cyrus in 529 BC (2 Chronicles 36: 23; Ezra 1: 2-4). However this cannot be the decree in question as it refers only to the Temple, not to the city. The second royal decree was made by Ataxerxes in 458 BC (Ezra 7: 11-26), but again no specific mention is made of rebuilding the city or its walls. Irrespective, Ezra himself evidently saw this decree as providing a broad approval, as he later thanked God in Ezra 9: 6-15 for extending His grace: "**He has extended grace to us in the presence of the Persian kings, giving us relief, so that we can rebuild the house of our God and repair its ruins, to give us a wall in Judah and Jerusalem**" (verse 9).

The third royal decree involving the Jews and their city was issued by the same Ataxerxes in 444 BC (Nehemiah 2: 5-8; 17-18) and specifically authorises the rebuilding of the city walls. Daniel's text in chapter nine indicates that this 'rebuilding' will persist until an 'anointed one' shall come – we have emboldened the relevant text above. Many Bible translations render *the anointed one* directly as 'the Messiah'. We think this interpretation is correct – it being impossible to think of anyone else it might mean.

The time period begins with the command to restore and build Jerusalem. The sixty nine weeks culminate with "the anointed one" (Messiah). But why a separate mention of seven weeks? The answer is expressed in the last words of verse 25: "**It will be rebuilt with a plaza and a moat, but in difficult times**". The seven weeks that precede the sixty-two weeks is generally considered to be the time period it took Ezra, Nehemiah and others to rebuild the city. For reasons too complex to enter into here, commentators opine that the rebuilding probably concluded in Darius' reign[8]. The sixty-two weeks plus the seven weeks brings us to the time of "the anointed one, the ruler" (or "Messiah the Prince", depending on translation used). This Messiah will be "cut off" and "will have nothing". Christian scholars have long accepted that the sixty-nine "weeks" (483 years) ended in the days of Yeshua (Jesus).

The text tells us that after sixty-nine weeks (7+62) Messiah is "cut off". It does not tell us that the seventieth week happens straight after the sixty-ninth week. Bible chronologists generally take either AD30 or AD33 as the year of Christ's

---

8 See e.g. "The Daniel Papers" by Martin R. De Haan II, Radio Bible Class Publishers 1994.

crucifixion (the earliest date would be AD27, and Peter Sammons tends towards this view). So adding 483 years to the 458BC date brings Jesus' crucifixion to – with certainty – the late twenties or early thirties of the Christian era.

The majority of serious Bible scholars are satisfied that the 483 years coincides with the end of the ministry of Jesus – and specifically when He affirmed that He is the Messiah and consequently was "cut off", or crucified. We note that some Jewish scholars have attempted other "explanations" so as to "find" another victim who is not Yeshua, but overall their explanations lack consistency and arguably are rather too liberal with alteration of original texts. Such matters are well beyond the scope of this book and readers can undertake their own detailed research if they need to. Your author accepts the "obvious" explanation as being consistent with the entire witness of Scripture and God's Salvation plan – the anointed one Who is cut off is the Lord Jesus, and He is cut off by crucifixion.

The declaration that Messiah will be cut off and have nothing needs no manipulation to be understood as a reference to the Lord's crucifixion. The Hebrew word translated as "cut off" refers to the execution of wrongdoers (Leviticus 7: 20; Psalm 37: 9; Proverbs 2: 22). Christians understand this as being most appropriate because, according to the apostle Paul, God made Messiah "to be sin for us" (2 Corinthians 5: 21). Although He had never sinned, Jesus died as a wrongdoer to pay the price for *our* sin – even His death by crucifixion was that of a criminal. Christians see the expression "will have nothing" as reflecting the reality that Jesus died apparently without followers or possessions. It seemed to onlookers at the time that He was an utterly defeated, dismal failure.

A blessed new age?

There is a problem! Even those who accept Jesus' crucifixion, as above, have to acknowledge that His resurrection did not usher in the golden age anticipated in Daniel 9: 24. Indeed this is a very clear objection amongst religious Jews to the reality of a crucified Saviour and to the claims of Yeshua as the Jewish Messiah. Up to this point, today, Yeshua has not "finished transgressions" nor made "an end to sins", nor apparently brought in "everlasting righteousness". We need to bear in mind, however, that in one sense all these things *have* been achieved, whilst in another sense they are yet to be fully realised.

We can say straightway that Yeshua did "**make reconciliation for iniquity**" through His sacrificial death. Through this, Christians see that He has achieved atonement and put an end to the Temple-based sacrificial system – and here

Jews must also acknowledge that today they have no Temple, nor do they have a publicly acknowledged and God-approved priesthood[9]. So Jesus has made reconciliation for sins and, we might add, that within His Kingdom indeed He *has* put an end to "transgressions", made an "end to sins" and brought in "everlasting righteousness" amongst His Own followers. These things have been a reality for virtually 2,000 years, albeit unacknowledged and unrecognised by the world at large. The final outworking of these prophecies lies in the future, but it is surely coming! The Gospel of Salvation is triumphant!

When, then, will the full realisation of all those things which Daniel predicted *actually* happen in a *universal* sense? Christians see two elements to this: (1) temporally when Jewish people finally and gladly receive their Messiah en-masse and (2) eternally when the new heaven and the New earth is inaugurated. Daniel 9: 24 begins "Seventy weeks are decreed about **your** people and **your** holy city". Plainly there is something in this about the Jewish people, although it might equally be applied to those grafted-in to that enlarged, Holy people. The sixty-ninth week has ended, but the seventieth has not yet begun. It is after seventy weeks that the fullness of God's blessings will come.

As we explored elsewhere in this book, the term "last days" encompasses the entire period from Pentecost until the Lord's second coming. All these presently are the last days, all these together constitute the 'last chance saloon' for Mankind. From this understanding, everything in Daniel 9: 26-27 that follows Messiah being "cut off" is part of Mankind's end times, and in these verses Daniel describes what happens *after* the 69th week has ended but *before* the 70th week begins. Then, Daniel highlights the events of this seventieth week:

After the anointed One has been "cut off" the peoples of a coming 'ruler' will destroy Jerusalem: "**The people of the coming ruler will destroy the city and the sanctuary. The end will come with a flood, and until the end there will be war**" (verse 26). This new hostile 'ruler' or 'prince' is likely to be "the little horn" of Daniel 7: 8 and 24-26 who makes war on the Saints until the Ancient of Days intervenes. This "ruler", it appears, will head a restored Roman Empire in the end times. Allowing that it was ancient Rome that "cut off" the Messiah and destroyed Jerusalem in AD70, it is not unreasonable to perceive a continuation of this power structure with a future role. In the past thirty years some Bible expositors have perceived a role for the European Union as the revived Roman Empire. Whilst there may be some validity and value in this idea it may, in fact,

---

9 Some wonder whether a "Third Temple" will be built in Jerusalem and a revived temple 'priesthood' conjured-up. This certainly seems to be a possibility but no such 'priesthood' could ever prove its legitimacy nor its Israelite tribe-affiliation. If a Third Temple is ever built therefore, it will not be a part of God's plan – but it may well be a part of Mankind's plans as Mankind seeks to syncretise religions and find 'political' solutions to its pressing problems.

be a considerable oversimplification of geopolitical (and spiritual) realities. Rome certainly destroyed Jerusalem in AD70. The phrase "**The end will come with a flood, and until the end there will be war; desolations are decreed**" perhaps points to both the destruction of Jerusalem in AD 70 *and* to the final end of our present age, which will come suddenly and overwhelmingly. Until that end, wars and rumours of wars will scar human history and "desolation", especially in relation to Daniel's people and to his city, will continue. Sadly, persecutions against the Jewish people have rarely ceased in our world.

The seventieth week will begin when someone with authority will make a binding commitment with a group of people called the "many". After 3.5 years he will break his agreement, accompanied by some sort of sacrilege against God. But finally the person who breaks this treaty and engages in that abomination will come crashing down. Daniel 9: 27 gives us the grim picture: "**He will make a firm covenant with many for one week, but in the middle of the week he will put a stop to sacrifice and offering. And the abomination of desolation will be on a wing of the temple until the decreed destruction is poured out on the desolator.**" This suggests, possibly, a reconstituted Jerusalem Temple (but we cannot be dogmatic about this) with its associated "sacrifices".

It seems clear that this seventieth week does *not* follow on immediately from the sixty-ninth. The picture is becoming clearer now: Daniel's time period of seven weeks plus sixty two weeks extends *from* the decree to restore Jerusalem *to* the Anointed One (Messiah). It is *after* this time period of 49 years plus 434 years that the Messiah is "cut off" and the city and its sanctuary is destroyed. Both events are well enough attested historically. The events cited in Daniel 9: 27 have not happened in the past, so we conclude they must lie in our future. Let's restate it: "**He will make a firm covenant with many for one week, but in the middle of the week he will put a stop to sacrifice and offering. And the abomination of desolation will be on a wing of the temple until the decreed destruction is poured out on the desolator.**" The man who 'will make a firm covenant with many for one week' is undoubtedly the ruler we have already encountered in verse 26. As we suggested, he is the "little horn" of Daniel 7, and the (presently) most common interpretation of this is that he will lead a western confederacy of nations, the revived Roman Empire in its "ten toes" of Daniel 2: 40-43 or "ten horns" of Daniel 7: 24. The same man is referred to as the Antichrist (1 John 2: 18) and as "the beast" (Revelation 13: 1-10).

The beast will apparently pose as a friend of Israel, giving Jewish people a sense of security and allowing them freedom to worship in their newly reconstituted Temple. Revelation 13 opens with this man receiving the adulation of all Mankind, having unified the Western world. He will have brought some form of order out of political and social chaos and people will feel duly grateful, even seeing him as a 'saviour' (perhaps in the same way that many Germans perceived Hitler as a 'saviour' in the years 1933 to 41). But later he drops all pretence and reveals himself as Satan's enforcer; he blasphemes God and wages war "against the saints to conquer them" (Rev 13: 6-7). From this point of revealing, he remains in power for 42 months before his spectacular and emphatic downfall.

The final statement of Daniel 9: 27 is difficult to translate. The Christian Standard Bible (cited above) aims for authenticity but here perhaps lacks clarity. The NIV is more helpful in this regard: "**at the temple he will set up an abomination that causes desolation, until the end that is decreed is poured out on him**". This seems to capture the essence of what transpires. Three New Testament passages throw light on this: Matthew 24:15; 2 Thessalonians 2: 3-4; and Revelation chapter 13 in its entirety. We have the sense that *the image of the beast* is erected in a reconstituted Jerusalem Temple and that all people will be compelled to worship it. This is the abominable event that will trigger the desolation of the Temple and the city of Jerusalem at the end of the age. The beast/Antichrist meets his doom in Daniel 11: 40-45 – and there is perhaps a just symmetry here – the Antichrist meets his end with no one to help him, just as Jesus died on a cross with no one to help Him.

The last point we should make here is that Israel received her true Messiah in this seventieth week. Daniel 12: 1-3 summarises what will happen to the Israelis as a nation:

> **At that time Michael, the great prince who stands watch over your people, will rise up. There will be a time of distress such as never has occurred since nations came into being until that time. But at that time all your people who are found written in the book will escape. Many who sleep in the dust of the earth will awake, some to eternal life, and some to disgrace and eternal contempt. Those who have insight will shine like the bright expanse of the heavens, and those who lead many to righteousness, like the stars forever and ever.**

At that time seems to refer to the interval between the rise of the Antichrist and his destruction. This time of great troubles for the world - "the Great Tribulation" in common parlance - is also a time of special trouble for the world's Jewish communities (Deuteronomy 4: 30; Jeremiah 30: 7; Matthew 24: 21-22) but they are not to be totally destroyed. Many Jews will turn and receive their Saviour, and Zechariah 12 graphically foretells God's supernatural deliverance of the surviving Israelis[10] at the close of this dreadful time:

"Then I will pour out a spirit of grace and prayer on the house of David and the residents of Jerusalem, and they will look at me whom they pierced. They will mourn for him as one mourns for an only child and weep bitterly for him as one weeps for a firstborn" (Zechariah 12: 10).

In conclusion

Jewish people who at this late stage still refuse to accept Yeshua will be removed in judgment (Ezekiel 20: 33-38). We conclude therefore that all Jewish people, Israelis or of the diaspora, who enter into the full blessings of this Kingdom age will be true Believers in Yeshua ha Massiasch (Jesus the Messiah). The Apostle Paul seems also to perceive this truth when he announces to the apostolic Roman church that "all Israel will be saved" (Romans 11: 26). Whilst the precise meaning of this is a subject of debate, yet it seems that a very large majority of Jews will receive their Messiah, just as Zechariah prophesied.

This has been a long chapter in our book, but we think readers will agree that Daniel's ninth chapter requires careful exegesis. We hope we have brought some 'light' into this complex subject. Readers are encouraged to undertake their own investigation of this matter as we have certainly not said all that can be said! We recommend however that readers do not rush at this. It is a study that requires years of prayer, bible searching, contemplation and stepping out in faith. The purpose of these exercises is not to satisfy our curiosity. Rather, it is to make us better disciples of the Lord, Yeshua, and Believers who are better prepared to face the future that inevitably must arrive, sooner or later. The future will not be comfortable, yet it *will* be glorious and we need to remain focused.

Our last word of advice to our readers is to be wary of Christians who are overly divisive on these complex matters and who have their own fully explained "systematic theology" on these matters. Such people all too often are hugely divisive and cause the good name of the Lord to be brought into disrepute. Bear in mind the clear warning of the Apostle Paul to Timothy: **"Warn them before God against quarreling about words. It is of no value, and only ruins those who listen"** (2 Timothy 2: 14 (NIV), see also Titus 3: 9 and Romans chapter 14 for perspective).

---

10 And presumably any Jews still living as a Jewish diaspora across the world

CHAPTER 12

THE CATCHING UP

avoid foolish controversies and genealogies and strife and disputes about the Law, for they are useless and worthless (Titus 3:9).

Enraptured?

In Luke 24: 51 we are told that, after Yeshua had ministered to the Disciples, He was taken up to heaven before their eyes – in other words they *saw* this and literally watched Him go. He was "taken up into heaven", an event that is now remembered by the simple term *the ascension*. In the ONMB[1] it is translated, "**while he was blessing them, He went away from them and He was being brought up into the sky**". The NRSV[2] says he was "carried up into heaven". In the Gospel of Mark a similar ending was added, some have argued, in later centuries. In the book of Acts, Luke repeats that Yeshua was taken up to heaven (1: 2 and 9). But Luke adds: "**They were looking intently up into the sky as he was going, when suddenly two men dressed in white stood beside them. "Men of Galilee," they said, "why do you stand here looking into the sky? This same Jesus, who has been taken from you into heaven, will come back in the same way you have seen him go into heaven**" (Acts 1: 10-11). The manner, then, of Messiah's departure from this world was plainly supernatural. It was meant to be – and it powerfully underscored that an old era was ending as a new one began.

As a writer I find it significant that what might have become a sort of reverie for the Disciples was cut short by the angel with a very practical question. He did not say: "why don't you now depart and develop plans for Easter and Christmas?", or indeed for saints days, clergy and laity, or theological colleges! His interjection was brief and highly practical. *Why are you looking into space?* He might have added, "your work starts here, and now". They (we) were being told that *we have work to do* and our principal task is not to sit around waiting,

1 One New Man Bible
2 New Revised Standard Version

but to fulfill Yeshua's "great commission" to His Church – it is all about sharing the good news of the Kingdom . . . The angels, however, added their intriguing statement: **"Jesus, who has been taken from you into heaven, will come back in the same way you have seen him go".** As we have already explored in chapter 7, Messiah's return will be visible, definitive, and supernatural. And it will be singular, in other words He will come back once.

If there is a subject that has caused great hurt in the Churches, as well as confusion amongst the Saints[3], it is one that first emerged as a thoroughly divisive matter in the 1830s. It is not our purpose here to recapitulate history and controversy that others have explored so well. But in the briefest terms the angst arose from a short passage in Paul's first letter to the nascent Thessalonian church. It alludes to the future and to the Lord's return to *this* world. The passage in question is 1 Thessalonians 4: 16 – 5: 4

> **"For the Lord himself will come down from heaven, with a loud command, with the voice of the archangel and with the trumpet call of God, and the dead in Christ will rise first. After that, we who are still alive and are left will be caught up together with them in the clouds to meet the Lord in the air. And so we will be with the Lord forever.**
>
> **Therefore encourage one another with these words. Now, brothers and sisters, about times and dates we do not need to write to you, for you know very well that the day of the Lord will come like a thief in the night. While people are saying, "Peace and safety," destruction will come on them suddenly, as labour pains on a pregnant woman, and they will not escape. But you, brothers and sisters, are not in darkness so that this day should surprise you like a thief".**

Plainly Paul is giving the Thessalonians some vital information here, but it is notable that, as a biblical text, this is all too often severed from its context, and we remember David Pawson's pithy comment that "a verse taken out of context is a pretext".

As a writer I do not accuse Christians of *deliberately* obfuscating this, but many have inadvertently done so. So our first comment must be that Paul's clear directive about the future was delivered in the context of ordinary people wondering what happens after death and what has happened to their loved ones. The purpose of Paul's text is not principally some sort of exposé of the future, it is principally a statement of comfort to those who have lost loved

---

3 Not to mention confusion amongst non-Christians

ones and are seeking assurance about the future of those loved ones. In that context there is an ordering of resurrection, and Paul has given it.

The good news in 1 Thessalonians for all Believers is that we can indeed have assurance, that those who have died "in Christ" will be *the first* to be resurrected, implying that those who have determinedly died "outside Christ" will be resurrected later – at the time of judgment. The reason why there is this early resurrection is not stated clearly in the passage, although we have the intriguing comment from Paul in 5: 1 that **"about times and dates we do not need to write to you"**. Whilst some would say this is a reflection of the Lord's own words *that none know the day or the hour* (not even the Son) but only the Father, we think it can equally be read: *I don't need to tell you the time/date because you already have an insight into this.* If we believe that the Moedim have prophetic relevance both to the past and to the future, then we surmise that the Lord's return is likely to be in the autumn. What we decidedly do not know (yet) is the year thereof. As much (most?) of the early Thessalonian church was comprised of Jews, their knowledge of and insight into the Moedim would have been central to their life and religious praxis. Hence, even at that early stage there may have been a tacit understanding that the Lord's return would be at an autumn festival, *after the harvest has concluded.* Be that as it may, we rejoice in that wonderful, happy and glad good news that the dead in Christ will arise first.

I Thessalonians chapter 4 provides the clearest indication that we have about this *catching up* of the faithful at the time of Messiah Jesus' return. Whilst some have sought to make this into a central tenet of teaching, in the apostle Paul's Thessalonian context it is almost an incidental comment, or an afterthought, to the more pressing question as to *what happens to the dearly departed in Christ.*[4] Today, however, Paul's commentary in 1 Thessalonians has taken on 'a life of its own' in Christian theological circles, arguably to the detriment of the wider body, and to the amusement of the non-Christian world.

Rev Paul Langham in his lovely book "Understanding Revelation" includes a section on what has become commonly known as "the rapture". His arguments are put succinctly, and so we borrow them here, albeit we are not quoting directly. Rev Langham reminds us that those who die in Messiah Jesus will be resurrected just as Jesus was resurrected. The body in which we are raised will be recongnisably us, albeit in a renewed and perfected form – we will know

---

4 It is helpful to read 1 Thessalonians chapter 4 in the light of 1 Corinthians chapter 15, especially vv 1-28. The Corinthians, evidently, were also challenged by the nature of resurrection and its timing. In verse 23-26 Paul reminds the Corinthian Believers that Messiah Jesus is the "firstfruits" of the resurrection – so making a direct allusion to the Moed of Firstfruits. Again Paul makes the point that the Lord returns (once) and then with him "those who belong to him".

and recognise each other, just as Jesus also was recognised by those who knew Him. Yet Jesus' body was simultaneously different – *the same but different!*

In the original Greek of 1 Thessalonians 4, the word used is literally to be "snatched up", or "caught up". It is reminiscent of the double meaning to the English word "transport", as in the idea of a "transport of delight". We recall the lovely old hymn "The King of Love my Shepherd Is"[5] which includes the poetic *"what transport of delight from thy pure chalice floweth"*. There has long been a wonderful truth around the idea that in the future we shall be 'transported' in a delightful way into the very presence of our Lord! By and large this "catching away" of true believers as indicated in 1 Thessalonians 4:17 *at the time of Messiah's return* is not disputed amongst Christians. What is disputed is the timing! When will it happen, and at what point in God's eschatological plan?

The great point at issue is the *timing* of this 'catching-up'. Broadly the controversy is around whether it happens before the great tribulation, or after it. As Rev Paul Langham says, it is significant that the key passage in 1 Thessalonians, which everyone acknowledges as being the major 'teaching' in this area, is not only silent on this point, it does not even display any awareness that there is a question to be answered. This apparent 'omission', here as elsewhere, is very significant. The apostle Paul did not think it necessary to spell out *when* this would be – a fact which Langham comments as "speaking volumes". It is in the minds of modern commentators where confusion exists, not in Scripture itself!

Let's pause for a moment to consider this word 'rapture'. Note that the word is not from our Bible, so an explanation of its derivation may be helpful. Our English *rapture* is widely assumed to be derived from Middle French *rapture*, via Medieval Latin *raptura* ("seizure, kidnapping"), in turn derived from the Latin *raptus* ("a carrying off"). Strangely, our modern word 'rape' comes from the same Latin root, *rapere*, which meant variously to "snatch, to grab, to carry off"[6]. From the 14th century, the term came to mean to "seize and take away by force". The Koine Greek of 1 Thessalonians 4:17 uses the verb form ἁρπαγησόμεθα (*harpagēsometha*), which means "we shall be caught up" or "taken away". The dictionary form of this Greek verb is *harpazō* (ἁρπάζω) and used also in texts such as Acts 8:39, 2 Corinthians 12:2–4, and Revelation 12:5.

Having considered the etymology of the word 'rapture', we can surely make a simple and straightforward interim conclusion based on the text in 1 Thessalonians chapter 4: when our Lord Jesus returns, for the true Believer that

---

5 Henry Williams Baker (1815-1877)
6 The dinosaur "raptor" comes from the same Latin root – here the meaning is "seizure" or "plunderer".

moment will be definitive, perhaps instantaneous and certainly a dramatic "snatching up", but this will not happen until those who have fallen asleep are first raised and brought *with* Jesus. The snatching up of the Believers alive at the time of Jesus' return will, as it were, complete the family totally – the church *triumphant* (to use an old term) will be united with the church *militant*. The dead in Christ, now raised, are joined by those alive in Messiah at the time of His return. A wonderful and glorious prospect, indeed! Our supernatural God who supernaturally created this world and supernaturally raised His Son from the garden tomb, will supernaturally – and literally – "raise" those who remain to be with Him, and to reign with Him. Our disbelieving World may balk or smirk at these ideas, but that is their problem, it is not God's problem; He has made this clear. But the clarity was brought to us in the context of *what happens to the already dead in Christ*, as opposed to what happens at the end of the present age. We repeat, it was a word of comfort to the mourning, rather than an exposé of the future.

When Jesus returns

As David Pawson points out in his splendid 270-page study "When Jesus Returns" (1995), there is no controversy amongst believing Christians in terms of this snatching up. The disagreement is fundamentally about timing and whether the Lord returns once, or twice, or conceivably even three times! At this point we must repeat what we said in chapter 1, the purpose of *this* book today is not to attempt to settle "theological" arguments. Our purpose here is to explore what the Bible actually says, not what others say that the Bible says!

Dispensational theology holds that Messiah Jesus will return to this world twice – firstly and secretly to 'rapture' true believers before the beginning of *the great tribulation*, and then a second time publicly to commence His millennial rule in this world. It must be said, however, that this teaching depends totally on a particular 'interpretation' of passages and verses, as the idea of a two-stage secret-public return is nowhere plainly taught in Scripture and can only be divined by reading-in[7] to Scripture certain fundamental tenets (or preconceptions). To put this most bluntly, these tenets are that Christians will inherit "heaven" eternally, and the Jews will inherit "the earth" eternally. Again we must comment, nowhere are these concepts plainly taught, and the ideas arose as late as the 1830s when they may have emerged from, or been stimulated by, a 'prophecy' by one Margaret Macdonald in Port Glasgow, Scotland. The precise

---

7 eisegesis

relationship of Macdonald to the early teachers of Dispensationalism, and the timing of her prophecy, is still a matter of considerable conjecture, so we shall invest no more time on it here. Perhaps the key point we *should* note is that prior to 1830 these teachings had no currency (of which we are aware) and this was not a mainstream, historic Christian teaching.

The last clear point to be made is that Dispensational theology teaches that Christians will escape that time which the Bible refers to as "the Tribulation". Yeshua spoke of this *time of trouble* in Matthew 24: 21. Jesus' revealing of the future to the Apostle John in Revelation 7: 14 speaks specifically of "the great tribulation", but arguably this reference could equally reflect more broadly the incessant troubles suffered by Christians since the time of Pentecost. Do "Christians" escape, then, the great troubles of which Jesus spoke? Your author feels that this idea, whilst superficially attractive, is incorrect, and understands that true Believers will go through the Tribulation *but be preserved within it*, until Messiah returns. We shall not be preserved intact, in the sense that there will be no losses nor martyrs. Quite the opposite, anti-Christian persecution will be reminiscent of, and more widespread than, any previous persecution. Yet it will not, we feel, be "worse" than previous. There is a sense in which "tribulation" has been a fellow traveler with Christians since Pentecost, sometimes waxing, at other times waning, but always *there in reality* and in daily experience. Not for nothing does the apostle Paul refer to us as "strangers" and "sojourners" in this world, who yearn for a better place (Ephesians 2: 19-20). Paul similarly refers to believers as "ambassadors", implying that we are in a real sense living in a land that is not our own (2 Corinthians 5: 20). Not for nothing did our Lord teach us to pray "thy Kingdom come" because this world is, and always has been, actively hostile to the witness of Jesus. We might say, believers truly have an investment and a stake in that future, which shall be the yet to be fully-realised and fully- empowered, Kingdom of God.

Rather than explore the varying and vying "theologies" that seek to describe and delineate *the snatching away* and its timing, we wish now to present what we believe to be a simple and straightforward understanding of Scripture as it pertains to these things. In doing so we deliberately distance ourselves from much of the 'controversy', mindful of the biblical injunction that Christian disputes are the "**ruin of those who listen**" (2 Timothy 2: 14 specifically; also Titus 3: 9 and Romans 14 (all)). In other words these intra-Christian disputes serve to turn people away from Jesus rather than towards Him.

Let us highlight what we think are the key elements of this:

- the Lord will return, once, at the absolute crisis point in world history when the devil will be in effective control
- this return will inaugurate the millennial rule of Yeshua ha Massiasch (Jesus the Messiah)
- for a period of (approximately, or specifically) 1,000 years Yeshua will rule. His rule will not be universally welcomed amongst Mankind, although it is likely that at first He will be seen for what He is, Saviour and sustainer, and One Who rules in righteousness – a huge change and difference from the previous rulership in this world that can be summarised in one word – Babylon
- at the end of 1,000 years there will be a final rebellion
- after that rebellion and its put-down, Yeshua and His chosen people will "tabernacle" together into eternity, in a new heaven and a new earth – which in reality are not two destinations, they are one.

The sober truth in this is that Christians must prepare, everywhere, for active and real persecution. The institutions that call themselves "church" will be largely apostate in these end times, so they will not teach about the reality of suffering, nor prepare their flocks to face it. Rather these 'churches' will identify (wholeheartedly?) with the World and with its agendas. Are we beginning to see this today? The remnant church (perhaps this would be better called the remnant *assembly*) will experience and undergo persecutions that will be reminiscent of the persecutions of all previous eras.[8] Whilst many will suffer, God's people will not be totally defeated and hence there will be faithful Believers for whom the Lord will return.

Building upon our earlier schematic of the Moedim we can visualise what we have been discussing in this way:

---

8 One question neither asked nor answered by "pre-trib rapturists" is why did God not, in earlier generations, and indeed does not today, rescue all true Believers from persecutions that lead to death? As He has not done this in the past, why would He do it secretly at the end?

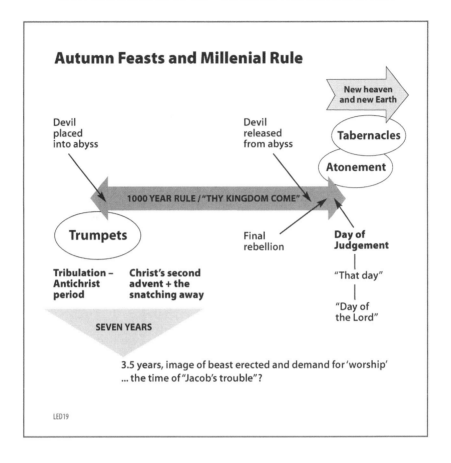

Autumn Feasts and Millenial Rule

New heaven and new Earth

Tabernacles

Atonement

Devil placed into abyss

Devil released from abyss

1000 YEAR RULE / "THY KINGDOM COME"

Trumpets

Final rebellion

Day of Judgement

"That day"

"Day of the Lord"

Tribulation – Antichrist period

Christ's second advent + the snatching away

SEVEN YEARS

3.5 years, image of beast erected and demand for 'worship' ... the time of "Jacob's trouble"?

LED19

This schematic is a 'close-up' of the final three autumn feasts in their prophetic revelation of the millennial rule. Whilst some may hold to an assumption they all happen at roughly the same time, Scripture itself reveals something different if we accept that the millennial rule is literal – remember Jesus shall reign *in this world* as Messiah. The *prince of peace* will have become the King of this world.

At the end of the Tribulation, Satan is incarcerated in 'the abyss'. We do not know in practical terms what this incarceration entails, or where/what is the abyss. We *do* know that the devil will be out of the picture for a very long time. After the final rebellion is put down, then judgment of the devil and all those who have, as it were, died *in him*, will take place. Atonement is all about forgiveness and it seems that, at this final Atonement, all those who have died and lived in Messiah Jesus will be 'judged' and yet acquitted on the basis of Yeshua's finished work on the Cross, *and solely on that basis*. This is salvation by grace – it is not in any way salvation by works.

All those that have lived and died in rebellion against Yeshua will then be judged, equally, and receive the fruit of their rebellions – they will be consigned alongside the devil to the dustbin of history. We should say two things about this consignment to the dustbin. First, the devil it appears will have no more power in the dustbin than any other rebel incarcerated there. The idea that Hell is where the devil rules is false; no such indication is given in Scripture. Second, in a sense all those granted their *earned* place in Hell get what they always wanted – they are "god" over their own eternity. True, they are "god" over nothing, with only themselves to blame. True, there is no 'communion' in Hell – Hell is not a community, nor are there spiritual or social interactions. Both the devil and all those who have sided with him have achieved their aim, yet the reality of that 'achievement' is self-torment and self-regret. All this is why the 'day of judgment' is so terrible as well as so wonderful (Matthew 12:36; also Revelation 20:11-15 , Hebrews 9:27, 1 Corinthians 4:5 , Romans 14:10, 2 Corinthians 5:10).

What does all this mean?

In the schematic above the catching away is depicted on the left. So Messiah returns at the crisis of world history. If God did not intervene at this point then the world itself would not survive and nor would God's remnant church.

Our diagram below shows how the seven years of 'tribulation' is split into two. For the final three and a half years, the Beast has to be worshipped. We assume that at this point life will become effectively impossible for the remnant church, but somehow true Believers[9] will be preserved, although many will be martyred. In some senses this may be reminiscent of, or analogous to, the Shoah which impacted the Jewish communities of the 1930s to 1940s; many killed but a remnant preserved. It also suggests a real symmetry in the visceral experience of persecution by Jew and Gentile.

---

9 whether Jewish or Gentile

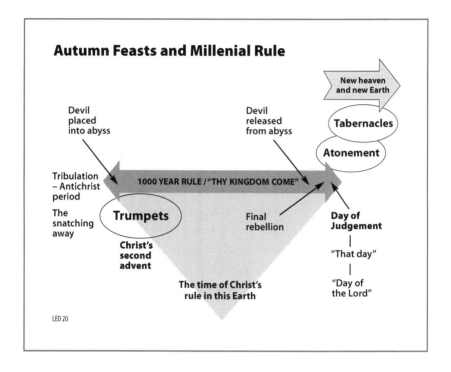

By this understanding the second coming happens once (as indicated in Scripture). How the final rebellion manifests itself is not described in the Bible; we must trust where we cannot trace. But we do know that Messiah's rule will not be universally popular and that He will rule "with a rod of iron" (yes, people will have received and been blessed by the perfect rule that they always demanded of God, and yet still they resent it – or at least some of them do). We are given no indication that Messiah is "absent" at the time of the final rebellion, so there is no need for a second, 'second coming'. Yet the rebellion will be put down finally and permanently.

This understanding encourages us that God's Word is faithful and true – and as relevant today as it has been in all previous eras. Previous generations of Christians have experienced many and egregious tribulations, as they do also today and will do tomorrow. The Lord will return and *catch up* His faithful people, and thereafter they shall rule with Him. There will be one visible and dramatic return of Messiah – and the world at large will be it seems relieved, rather than glad, to encounter its Saviour in the flesh. Christians will not, however, escape tribulation; rather we shall be sustained through it. It will be a terribly hard time and some will abandon their faith. Others will be martyred, and yet others will be preserved. When our Lord returns He will be accompanied by the 'church triumphant' i.e. all those who have died in Christ.

And He will be met and worshipped by the still-alive 'church militant', snatched up physically to be in His presence.

Of course this is not the triumphalist[10] message that so many church people want to hear. Can we call people to come to saving faith in a God whose people will suffer so? The answer here assuredly is . . . yes! Partly because the gospel message is today the same as it was 2,000 years ago. What saved then will save today. What saved those who had to suffer Nero's flames and Nero's lions in the first century AD, will sustain and save us today – and tomorrow. As our world progressively unravels and becomes ever more God-averse, and God-opposed, so we can say with confidence (whether we are believed or not) that *Scripture and prophecy is being fulfilled*. The message we must give will still be that of the apostle Peter: "**save yourself from this corrupt and evil generation**" (Acts 2: 40). Whether people act upon this instruction is ultimately up to them. Our urgent task remains to proclaim. It seems that many, many millions will hear and "turn" because during these years of trouble the Beast will progressively be recognised and revealed, until finally he will show himself for who he really is, demanding worship. We are to fear Him Who can consign body and soul to Hell rather than him who can destroy the body but not the soul (Matthew 10: 28). Our God reigns and He is coming, first for His saints and then to rule in righteousness.

144,002

In this book we make the clear connection between the *last days* and the *end time*. The purpose of this book is certainly not to decipher all the questions and difficulties associated with the End Time – that is, the very end of the last days and the time of Yeshua's return to this world. In the book of Revelation we encounter two complex questions that your author decided largely to ignore, not because they are unimportant but because to explore and resolve each would surely require at least a separate book between them, and *this* book is already long enough! Furthermore *this* book is not a treatise on the book of Revelation and numerous excellent writers have sought to shed light into these areas (see the further reading section at the end of this book for some suggestions).

Complex question No 1 is the identity of the 144,000 of Revelation Chapter seven who are "sealed" as God's final witnesses in this world. Who are they, and is the number 144,000 to be read literally or symbolically (or both)? Complex

---

10 or escapist?

question No 2 concerns the two witnesses of Revelation 11: 3-12. Who are they, and how is their witnessing to be understood? The answer we shall give now is necessarily brief and we shall not try to 'defend' our position. We acknowledge there are a number of different 'interpretations' of what will transpire in the future, some of which have wide currency amongst Christians. Once again your author states clearly that he finds many of these 'standard' explanations questionable, and/or weak. To that extent they are unsatisfactory.

Given that the Lord's return shall be at the end of the Tribulation period and this event presages the Millennial Rule of Messiah Jesus, and given that the 'catching up' involves the *church militant* being linked directly to the *church triumphant* and then 'coming' *together* with Yeshua, we understand the events around the 144,000 of Revelation chapter 7 and the two witnesses of Revelation chapter 11 to be events tied-in with the Tribulation. In our schematic "autumn feasts and millennial rule" (above) we consider both these elements to happen in the second half of the Tribulation period (but we are not dogmatic about this, and we have not included this detail within those schematics). There are numerous 'interpretations' of these two aspects of Revelation and it is recommended that the diligent reader seek out good exegetical work on the book of Revelation. For the record, however, we confirm our view as follows.

As regards the number 144,000 . . . a veritable 'industry' of interpretation has arisen since, in particular, the 1830s. On the Dispensational side of interpretation there is a developed theory that the 144,000 are sealed so that they can witness for (or be missionaries to the world for) the Lord during the time of Tribulation. However a plain reading of the text makes no such claim. This is likely, therefore, to be a perspective driven principally by *eisegesis*.

Since theologians and commentators on all sides of the hermeneutical spectrum broadly accept that the book of Revelation is saturated with symbolism, the clear task of the exegete is to try to establish what is purely symbolic, what is literal and what may simultaneously be both. The outcome of their deliberations will be determined, in part, by whether they consciously or subconsciously apply a "Greek" or a "Hebraic" mindset to the question[11]. Your author attempts to apply a Hebraic insight when exploring Scripture – after all, the Bible is largely a Jewish product, so a Jewish insight is nothing if not helpful to this!

Some opine that the 144,000 are specifically and solely Jewish Messianic

---

11 UK writer Steve Maltz has probably done more than any other modern writer to explore specifically these two mindsets and how they impact and influence hermeneutics. His books are rather too numerous to cite in full and all tend to explore this foundational question. However his book "Hebraic Church" is possibly the most relevant in this specific area and widely available at the time *this* book was completed in 2022.

believers who act as global missionaries in the end time. People holding this idea cite Revelation 7: 4 as a 'proof' verse, however there is no *extended* biblical text that develops or further explains this view. The idea also seems to depend on the belief that non-Jewish believers will have already been 'raptured' away (see earlier in this chapter) at this point in time. The number 144,000 can be argued as highly symbolic. Also, the fact that those 'sealed' are all identified as *of the tribes of Israel* contains its own story. If Christians can be defined as honorary Jews, then are they, in a spiritual sense, 'sons' of all the tribes of Israel? The 'sealing' of the 144,000 may then indicate, once again, that God preserves throughout all the trouble-filled ages of the last days, a people whom are 'preserved' within those troubles and whom, whether they live or die in the faith, are preserved for eternity as God's elect.

Be that as it may, we must note that the 'sealing' happens between the sixth and the seventh bowl being emptied upon the Earth, so there does, indeed, seem to be an ordering of this in an historical and revelatory sense. On that basis there is 'room' for the idea that, irrespective of tribe affiliation (which must be a closed matter in our era – no one really knows the tribes, only God does), the 144,000 may literally be Jewish Believers specially empowered at a given point in time. Your author here is not dogmatic about this and cannot see any real 'profit' or value in dogmatism; in this revelatory number God's Spirit may simultaneously be speaking to us at a number of different levels. As regards the 144,000, on prayerful reflection, your author tends towards the views:

- Likely to be Jewish Messianic believers (Jewish, as tribes are specifically cited), and apparently distinct from the wider community of surviving Believers – if we cross-reference Revelation passages including especially chapter 12)
- The number is probably symbolic (seven 'churches' cited in Revelation, but many more are not specifically listed, for example)
- The 144,000 are not evangelists! This view assumes something called a 'pre-tribulation rapture' (see above) and assumes that "Christians" will already have been 'rescued' from trouble, leaving Jews to 'face the music'. Whilst we understand this view, we do not find it compelling.
- The 144,000 may be literal and metaphorical at the same time, speaking to us at more than one level

Moving on to consider the two witnesses of Revelation chapter 11, once again we find definite 'room' for these to be considered at more than one level, and both literally and symbolically *at the same time*. This becomes easier to understand once one accepts that the book of Revelation is not a linear, time-sequenced exposé of the future, but that it recapitulates and explores the same themes in multiple different ways. The two witnesses are opposed by all those things we understand as "the World", that is everything that is opposed to God and to His purposes. Another word redolent of all this is *Babylon*. There are two key insights or 'theories' to this and your author considers these insights are not opposed, they are different but both likely to be true, simultaneously. The first is that the two witnesses are collectively Jewish believers in Jesus and Gentile believers in Jesus; though one family they remain distinct in witness and in service. Both will be opposed by the World until the End, at which point momentarily they will appear to be defeated and, consequently, the opposing World system ('Babylon') will rejoice. The second is that the two witnesses are real individual people, whose identity is not made plain by Scripture. We can speculate on identity, but speculation is only. . . speculation! Our considered view of the two witnesses, in brief:

- Likely to be two actual people.
- Identity speculative. The argument that neither Enoch nor Elijah died and that "man is appointed to die once", and both were preachers of righteousness is an intriguing and persuasive one, but your author here remains cautious. The two witnesses do not *have* to be returning prophets or people from the past. Jesus referred to John the Baptist as "Elijah", when referring to the Spirit's work through him, but no one suggests that John was Elijah returned!
- We find it intriguing that they are "two olive trees". We follow the trail back to Romans chapter 11 (wild and natural olive branches), and then back to Zechariah chapter 4: a gold menorah with seven lamps (we think of Revelation's seven lampstands) and oil (symbolic of the Holy Spirit) flowing into them. Zerubbabel is symbolic of the Messiah – building and completing the temple of the Lord (v9), which the New Testament reveals to be the "one new man"[12] of "enlargement theology". Given that a Hebraic understanding of the Bible can often be *both* literal and symbolic simultaneously, we see the testimony of the two witnesses in Revelation as also being the combined testimony to the World of the Jewish people through the Tanakh and the witness of Believers, or perhaps more accurately the witnesses of Jewish and Gentile Believers.

---

12 The inspiration of the useful *One New Man Bible* translation – see further reading section of this book.

This is necessarily a quick summary of a hugely challenging and potentially complex (and divisive?) truth. We repeat, to truly and comprehensively open up these matters, is not merely the requirement for a new book, it is more likely the product of a lifetime of study, prayer, and reflection. Your author offers the above as his contribution[13], and feels that it ties-in with everything else explored and exposed in *this* book.

---

13 It must be said that other Christians hold broadly to these views, which are not unique to the author.

CHAPTER 13

THE MILLENNIAL RULE – PROJECTING FORWARD

Hear, O Israel! The LORD is our God, the LORD is one!
You shall love the LORD your God with all your heart
and with all your soul and with all your might.
These words, which I am commanding you today,
shall be on your heart (Deuteronomy 6:4-5).

at that time the sign of the Son of Man will appear in the sky,
and all the nations of the earth will mourn (Matthew 24:30).

Direct rule

In the 1970s during that sad time in UK history known as "the troubles" of Northern Ireland, government rule of Northern Ireland was transferred *from* the locally elected and devolved 'Executive' at Stormont (Belfast) *to* direct rule from Westminster, London. It was a sensible expedient at a time when there was a question-mark over the legitimacy of the elected Stormont administration and indeed its very ability to govern. The cleanest way to move forward was to impose temporarily direct rule from Central Government. Rule from Westminster, in any case, took a little of the sectarian heat out of Northern Ireland politics[1]. The Bible seems to give a clear picture of 'direct rule' by Christ over this world and in this chapter we seek to explore what the Bible says, and conversely, what it does not say.

In chapter 8 we used a schematic that sketched the outline of God's outworking of the final part of His salvation plan, repeated here for ease of use:

---

1   devolved rule was eventually re-established.

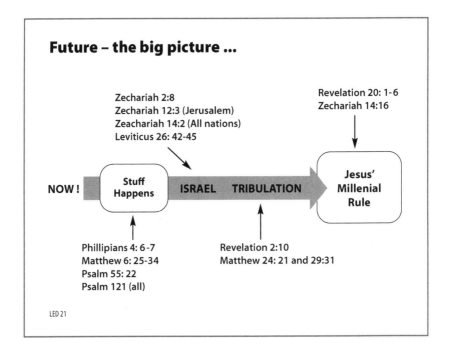

The sense conveyed here is that between now and the End Time a lot of history happens, but it is not random. It always reflects the reality that God is in control and our world is moving inexorably in a certain, defined, direction. That is what we mean by our cryptic comment, "stuff happens". We live our Christian lives faithfully and as best we can (in His strength, not in our own) and we depend on God for all things. Even so, the *world at large* goes its own way, charting its own course, largely ignoring its Creator God and so – *stuff happens!* The left to right arrow symbol depicts the progress of history/time. Between our 'now' and the future's 'then' there will be two key events denoting the approach of the end. Israel, as we have suggested throughout this book, plays a part in the End Time scenario, and tragically the world at large will "rise up" at a given point against Israel (Zechariah 14: 2). Either *before*, at the same time, or conceivably *after* the world intervenes as regards Israel, there will be a time of unprecedented simultaneous trouble across the world, which some Bible translations describe at *the great tribulation*.

The time of trouble (tribulation) is brought to a conclusion by Messiah's second advent into this world to begin what some call "the millennial age", or Christ's 1,000-years direct rule in this world. In *this* book thus far we have studiously rejected the 'traditional' Christian nomenclature for end-time scenarios, in large part because we believe that each of these, to greater or lesser extent, contain error and all are pretty much unintelligible to the 'average man or woman in the street'. Jesus spoke to ordinary people in ordinary language, so we should seek to do the same. At this point, however, we will quickly observe that most 'traditional' insights into the End Time revolve around varying interpretations of what is called *the millennial age*. These insights generate great heat, but often rather less light!

At this point your author wishes to make clear his understanding that in the future there will be a time of Christ's direct rule in this world and that this rule will follow, and be a consequence of, that time known as Armageddon – the world's penultimate war. Please refer again to our chapter 7 where we look at the return of Christ. Sufficient detail is given for us to have a degree of confidence in the assertions that "stuff happens", that Israel will be intimately involved in the end-time scenarios, and that there will be a millennial rule.

There is no universal, or even broad, consensus amongst Christians as to the precise ordering of these things. In chapter 7 we outlined the generally agreed truths around Christ's second coming. In this chapter your author clarifies for readers his understanding of these key truths, but does so with a genuine sense of humility, in that alternative interpretations presently do have wide currency, and these interpretations are held tenaciously by some who are truth seekers. We now set out *our* stall in the prayer that we might help others to gain greater confidence in the dependability of our God and His Word, and His loving-kindness . . .

Confederacy

A confederacy of nations is likely to emerge and direct its ire towards Israel. There may be other geo-political factors – and players – and it would be foolish for us to speculate too much on the precise details. Such discussions can be helpful and even instructive for the serious seeker after truth, but as we have said elsewhere, some things are being kept obscure by God until the End. This confederacy of nations will threaten Israel militarily but ultimately will be defeated in an entirely supernatural manner. After this, Messiah Jesus will return to reign upon His throne, located in Jerusalem.

What does the term *millennial reign* mean? Please note this term does not specifically occur in Scripture, something we too easily forget. The word "millennium" is from the Latin words mille and annum. Mille means one thousand. Annum means years[2]. When combined they mean one thousand years. The word

---

2 Strictly, Annus means 'year', Annos means 'years'.

"reign" means the time during which a sovereign reigns; royal authority is that period of time during which a king, queen, or emperor, is ruler of a country.

The words "a thousand years" or "the thousand years" are mentioned six times in Revelation 20: 1-7. Whilst in the Bible statements as regards time may not always be literal, in Revelation chapter 20 there seems no compelling reason to understand or interpret what is said in an allegorical or figurative sense. On that basis we take the text in its plain sense and understand this to be a literal 1,000-year rule. As to why this might "fit" with other plans of God we shall explore shortly. Assuming for a moment our understanding is correct (and indeed this is the understanding of a substantial number of Bible-believing Christians) then the Lord Jesus will be the sovereign King with all authority reigning physically in His earthly Kingdom. Remember, "thy Kingdom come, thy will be done . . ."

It seems that the Jerusalem Temple will have been re-erected at this time, or more likely shortly prior to Messiah's return. But must this be re-erected on the present Temple Mount? On this matter we must be reticent, noting for example that there is some dispute as to whether the Second Temple (Herod's Temple) was on the precise same site as Solomon's First Temple. And indeed, is God obliged to use precisely the same site, in any case? If the Temple is re-erected it will become effectively the Third Temple.[3] Some commentators suggest that Temple animal sacrifice will re-emerge, mimicking the Second Temple pattern. They think (or appear to think) that God will approve and instigate this. Your author here thinks this is highly unlikely as it is difficult to perceive any theological 'logic' in such a development since Messiah's sacrifice on the cross was once for all (Hebrews 9: 23 to 10: 18). Why would Jesus reinstitute a sacrificial system when He has already made the ONE acceptable sacrifice?

Those who argue for a reinstated Sacrificial system cite many Scriptures which they believe support their position. To evaluate these Scriptures in detail would be a huge task and unwieldy in this book. It is your author's considered view that these references confuse clear First Temple sacrificial instructions with a future scenario. We note that some Scriptures/prophecies mix near and far term truths (as we have said elsewhere) and we suspect that where texts/verses have been used to "justify" the idea of a resumption of animal sacrifice, that interpreters holding these views have failed to make that distinction. Furthermore, there are degrees of sacrifice besides animal sacrifice, so if God shall in future require sacrifice, why should it not be, for example, the sacrifice of a truly broken, penitent heart? Or the sacrifice or praise and worship? Or even the sacrifice of prayer, fasting and physical pilgrimage to a reinstated

---

3 Some suggest that the Older Tabernacle was also a "Temple" so any "new" End-Time Temple might legitimately be considered as the Fourth Temple!

Temple? Or a combination of these things?

Just one example will have to suffice: a current website[4] claiming that animal sacrifice must resume cites ten bible verses (or portions), and amongst these present Isaiah 56: 6-8 as evidence. Yet this portion is lifted out of its proper context. As the late David Pawson used to say, "a verse taken out of context is a pretext". So in Isaiah 56 the context is clearly one of Salvation, and indeed this chapter wonderfully tells us that Salvation is available to the "foreigner" as well as for Jews (56: 3). In this it surely anticipates the renewed ("new") covenant of Jeremiah 31: 31. Verses 6 to 8 of Isaiah 56 speak about *foreigners* coming to the Temple to worship, and in this it again anticipates the salvation of Gentiles alongside Jews. Yet Jesus Himself quoted Isaiah 56: 7 as He angrily overturned the money-lenders' tables in the Second Temple: "It is written," he said to them, "My house will be a house of prayer, but you have made it 'a den of robbers'" (Luke 19:46, NIV). So Jesus quoted Isaiah 56 within the precincts of the Second Temple, and He plainly saw it as applicable in His Own day. It is a huge stretch to say that it speaks of a *yet-to-be-built* Third Temple!

The problem here is, of course, the age-old one that you can make the Bible say whatever you require if you pick verses at random and sever them from their proper context. Going back to the idea of a future Temple animal sacrifice, your author thinks this is unlikely given the completed work upon the Cross. Of course it is possible that 'sacrifice' will be required in the millennial reign of Messiah, but a 'sacrifice' (as we have noted) does not have to be of an animal. Perhaps it will be the sacrifice of praise and worship. We emphasise, there is more than one type of sacrifice acceptable to God, but none can supplement or supplant the blood of Jesus. Prior to the return of Jesus it is entirely possible that the Beast-Antichrist will want to institute some form of blood sacrifice, but plainly such a move will not be of God.

If a Third Temple arises in Jerusalem, will this in fact be at the instigation of the devil, to facilitate his new global religion and global worship system that must arise? And will this in some way be linked to the false peace that the Bible foretells (Daniel 8: 23-25; Daniel 9: 27)? We think this is far more likely – so beware, Christian! We should be highly sceptical of all moves to reinstate Temple worship in Jerusalem. If Messiah Jesus really requires this, then no doubt He will make it plain upon His second advent at the end of this age. It is not for us to plot, scheme, engineer, or second-guess what God may do. God is more than capable of overruling!

---

4 We really do have to be mightily cautious about website 'scholarship'. There's an awful lot of rubbish out there!

Millennial rule

The Bible seems abundantly clear that when Messiah returns to this world He will be established as ruler in Jerusalem, sitting on the throne of David (Luke 1: 32–33). It is true to say that there are two key 'types' of Covenant in the Bible, those where God acts unilaterally and those where God requires a corresponding response from Mankind in order for Men to receive a corresponding blessing. Strictly speaking all covenants are *promulgations* in that God always takes the initiative, so they are never in any sense 'bargains' between God and Man. Nevertheless some Covenants are such that we can characterise them as *conditional* versus *unconditional*[5].

The unconditional covenants taken together (i.e. those that God institutes and do not require affirming actions on the part of Men (Mankind), and in particular the Abraham (land) covenant), presage a literal and physical return of the Messiah to establish His Kingdom. The Abraham Covenant promises to Israel a land, a posterity and a ruler, together with a spiritual blessing (Genesis 12: 1–3). The David Covenant promises Israel a king from David's line who is to rule forever – giving the nation permanent rest from all her enemies (2 Samuel 7: 10–13). At the second coming (second incarnation), these covenants will finally be fulfilled as Israel is *re-gathered* from the nations (Matthew 24: 31), *converted* (Zechariah 12: 10–14), and *restored* to the land under the rule of Messiah Jesus.

The Bible speaks of world conditions during the millennium as being a near perfect environment, both physically and spiritually. It will be a time of peace (Micah 4: 2–4; Isaiah 32: 17–18), joy (Isaiah 61: 7, 10), and comfort (Isaiah 40: 1–2). Furthermore it will be a time of obedience (Jeremiah 31: 33), holiness (Isaiah 35: 8), truth (Isaiah 65: 16), and the knowledge of God (Isaiah 11: 9, Habakkuk 2: 14). Messiah will rule as King (Isaiah 9: 3–7; 11: 1–10). Nobles and governors will also rule (Isaiah 32: 1; Matthew 19: 28), and Jerusalem will be the political centre of the world (Zechariah 8: 3). We say 'near perfect', above, because, as we shall shortly suggest, there will remain the potential (and reality?) of rebellion even in this beautiful social environment. Revelation 20: 2-7 gives a precise time period of the millennial kingdom. There are other passages that point to a literal reign of the Messiah in this world. The outworking of many of God's promises rests on a literal, physical, future kingdom. Whilst the term 'one thousand years' may not be literally one thousand *to the precise day* (and we note that the Bible can use timings in a

---

5 See Peter Sammons "The Messiah Pattern" Appendix 3 for a full exploration of this subject

figurative sense) there is no solid basis for denying the literal understanding of the millennial Kingdom and its duration being of 1,000 years. This, incidentally, is the Kingdom for which we express our yearning when we echo Jesus' words "Thy Kingdom come, Thy will be done on earth as it is in heaven".

Whilst the rule of God in this world will be perfect, and in a very real sense shall finally answer all those critics who try to blame God when things go wrong ("why doesn't God *do* something about this") His rule will not be universally welcomed. We have the intriguing statement in Revelation 2: 27 that Messiah's viceroys in this world will be authorised to rule "with a rod of iron" (repeated in 19: 15). This suggests that people will still have rebellious and wayward hearts even during the millennial rule, despite the fact that they will have seen with their own eyes the practical blessings and benefits of living by God's standards. In the equivalent prophecy of Zechariah we have the clear vision of our world *where the Lord reigns* (and your author understands this to be the time of Messiah's millennial rule). In this time the nations will go up, year by year, to celebrate the *feast of booths* (AKA Sukkot or Tabernacles). Precisely how they do this and how the nations are to be represented is not revealed by Zechariah's prophecy; once again we must say it is none of our business at this time, today. Intriguingly again, whichever nations fail to observe this act of worship of the Lord will suffer drought ("no rain") which, once more, suggests both the potential for rebellion and for consequent punishment (Zechariah 14: 16-18).

The scenario (or trigger event) that ultimately brings direct millennial rule seems to be that the World rises up against Israel and threatens to destroy her and, in the process, itself. This threat will occur towards the end of that time of "trouble" (or tribulation) which, had it not been cut short, would have destroyed all Mankind (Matthew 24: 22). The tribulation will only be brought to an end by Messiah's second coming, just in the nick of time. At this point all surviving believers will be "caught up" to be with Jesus[6]. These surviving believers, alongside believers from previous eras, will be God's agents in millennial rulership. We hope it does not sound trite or banal to suggest this may be a sort of Godly 'civil service' enacting the Messiah's direct instructions and indeed acting under 'delegated authority' in His Name.

Why will Jesus (need to) rule for 1,000 years? Here we must state plainly that the Bible gives no direct answer, nor does it even give an indirect answer! Your author speculates, however, that because Mankind will have made such a terrible mess of the world at every level through those events that the Bible characterises as 'tribulation' and culminating in 'Armageddon', so it may take

---

6 See chapter 12

Mankind several hundreds of years, acting under Messiah's direct rule, to clear up the mess that Mankind's rebellions have in the first place caused. At first, this time might be characterised by hard remedial work – and Mankind will be sufficiently content with this process as, collectively, it still holds a very clear memory of tribulation and of Armageddon, and of all that preceded it. Direct rule by Christ will seem a haven and an oasis by comparison. But memories inevitably fade, and future generations will increasingly resent direct rule – in other words the old problems of discontent and rebellion may begin to reassert themselves. If so, this suggests to us that the release of Satan from the Abyss (Revelation 20: 7-8) will mean once again, and finally, that the devil seduces Mankind into rebellion[7]. It may be that the period before the end of the millennial rule will look something like the period immediately before Christ's second coming. History repeating itself?

Other viewpoints

At this point we do not wish to explore the panoply of competing viewpoints. A helpful resource in all this is David Pawson's 270-page book "When Jesus Returns". As always, Pawson is careful to explore competing viewpoints before stating where he stands. His book is sub-divided into four sections, and the fourth he entitles "The Millennium Muddle". He describes six distinct approaches to the idea of Millennium and then confirms that his own view is what he has already described as "Classical Pre-millennialism". This is a view that, he says, takes a middle course between abject *pessimism* about the future and *naive optimism* which posits that this world will be progressively "Christianised" and that the great Tribulation will not happen.

Pawson says he takes Revelation 20 in its plainest sense and accepts the broad *sequence* of events as described in the book of Revelation. He goes on to state that "Classical" means that this view was the earliest commonly held belief of the Church. Notably, alternate views and 'interpretations' did not emerge until the Byzantine/Roman Catholic eras, under the heady and pervasive influence of Greek philosophy. Your author finds himself in close agreement with Pawson's broad position but does not wish to restate much of what Pawson taught. His books[8] are still widely available and (under God's

---

7 Others suggest that the release of Satan and final rebellion publically vindicates God's righteousness in eternal judgment. Even when Messiah rules and Satan is bound, the human heart remains rebellious. In this sense, Satan does not have to "seduce" Mankind because the human heart is fallen and thoroughly rebellious (Jeremiah 17: 9). Your author considers that this view also has merit.

8 His teaching videos are also freely available via e.g. YouTube.

providence) will likely continue to be so unless and until there is a widespread clamp-down on Christian literature in the English language.

An earlier Bible teacher, J. Oswald Sanders, states that the return of Christ is *a certain fact* clearly promised in Scripture. In his book "Certainties of Christ's Second Coming" (1977) he says that, although there are differing interpretations of some Bible passages, nevertheless many vital points remain beyond serious dispute amongst true Believers. In saying this Oswald Sanders echoes Joe Church in his book "Every Man a Bible Student", who also posits this broad and common understanding of our future, but without partisan dogmatism. We have incorporated the broad thrust of Joe Church's conclusions in our chapter 7. Oswald Sanders also holds to a Classical Pre-Millennial understanding, although that is not the term he uses.

Rev Paul Langham in his 192-page book "Understanding Revelation" also holds to a pre-Millennial understanding. In this he means (as do all the others) that we now live in a period that is *before* the millennial rule and that Christ will directly rule in *this* world. Langam's book remains commercially available at this time of writing and is to be commended on many grounds. One thing that Langham points out more clearly than other expositors is the truth that Revelation is not a linear prophecy as it persistently loops back on itself – it is in a sense, repetitive. This can make it hard to follow – certainly for the casual reader. We highly commend Langham's book as a brilliant introduction to the vital final book of the Bible.

Finally a good friend of author Peter Sammons is Philip Wren, a Bible student of many years and writer of the excellent "Revelations of Jesus Christ" – a devotional study of the book of Revelation. Wren's 163-page book draws a similar conclusion to the one we have just expressed. Firstly, Wren assumes the rule to be of 1,000 years (Sammons is content with the idea of *approximately* 1,000 years – a little less or a little more seems to him not to make much difference). Secondly Wren is more forthright in the idea of a second and final rebellion. He notes (page 133) that Jesus will rule with a rod of iron and cites Psalm 2: 8-9; Revelation 2: 26-27 and 12: 5 as he reflects upon this.

Philip Wren states (and in this we are leaning heavily on his text) that 'the final rebellion' vindicates the justice of God. In Ezekiel chapters 38 and 39 there is a description of a time when Gog and his hordes come up to attack Israel. Two events are being described in these chapters. The events are similar but have certain marked differences that set them apart in time. The separate events tie in with Revelation 19 and 20. In Revelation 19 there is an allusion to Ezekiel 39. *The birds are gathered to the supper of the great God.* It is the final rebellion against Christ coming to reign on the earth. Says Wren:

Revelation 20: 8 makes a more direct reference to Gog and Magog as in Ezekiel 38. At the end of this present age when Jesus returns to claim His throne the people of this world will reject His rule and gather to fight against Him. Following the victory of Christ, all the wicked are removed (Matt 13: 41). The population of the world, during the reign of Christ, will be made up of two peoples; Christ's brethren who have proved their loyalty and faithfulness, and the sheep who are, as we have seen, made up of 'good people'. At the end of the 1000 years the sheep are given a choice, as Satan is released to test them.

At last after 1,000 years they have a champion to stand against Christ. Many 'good people' and their descendants will reject the reign of Christ. His laws have been a burden to them. That is why we have two descriptions of the rebellion by Gog. The end of the coming age will be almost identical to the end of this present age. Both ages will end with a rebellion as Mankind resists the reign of Christ. The reign of Christ proves that even the 'good people' in reality hate His rule. All excuses that man makes as to why he disobeys God have now been answered. The citizens of the millennial Kingdom and all those who preceded them in the former ages, have one thing in common, "they love and practise a lie".

It is the same old lie that Eve fell for in the garden. It is Satan's constant lie that God does not want to give the best to His creation. Satan taunts, "listen to me and you will become like God". Such is the deceitfulness of man's heart, the number of those who are stirred by Satan to rebel is like the sand on the sea shore. They have experienced the reign of Christ and seen this world returned to its former paradise. Yet despite the benevolent reign of Christ they will not submit to Him. Instead they listen to Satan.

For a time men lived in a foretaste of the perfect Kingdom of God, yet it seems their one wish was to destroy it. It is the perfect justice of God that only those who *freely* choose to submit to His rule over their lives, can enter through the gates to the eternal city. Those who are outwardly good by the standards of this world but inwardly are in rebellion cannot and never will be able to enter. The judgment of Jesus has been vindicated. He is righteous and just. Worthy is the Lamb.

n.b. the above is not a direct quotation but a very close paraphrase of Wren's page 135. As with Pawson and Langham, we also highly commend Wren to our readers as they seek to dig-deeper.

In conclusion …

Of course in one chapter we have not plumbed all the beauties of the 1,000-year rule of Messiah Yeshua, and we acknowledge other viewpoints. We feel, however, that what we have presented here is a good broad-brush appreciation of what the future holds. We would go one step further, however. As we revert to our earlier schematic (see chapter 5), we can reinterpret it in this way: the first three Moeds lie in the past (crucifixion, burial and resurrection). The fourth is the era in which we live today[9] – it is the era of the eternal harvest, but this is an era that will have a definite end point, and that will be when the Lord returns.

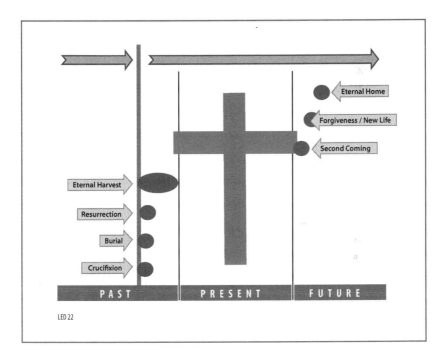

LED 22

The present era might well be called the Christian era, and we note the irony of the fact that secular scholars and commentators now seek to define our present era simply as "CE" as they try to erase and air-brush mention of Jesus from our civic discourse. "CE", which they call their "common era" might just as easily be called "Christian era", which is certainly not what they intend! Have they not paused to consider precisely what it is that makes our era "common" to all Mankind? The future era is the one we wish to focus upon now.

---

9 i.e., the "Last Days" as we defined these in Chapter 2

The final three Moeds illustrate the next three items on God's Salvation agenda, and they reflect these (surely?) in the precise order in which they are going to happen. Towards the end of the harvest period, Jesus will send urgent signals (shofar blasts) that His return "draws near". These signals will increase in frequency and intensity as we draw closer. The remnant church[10] will be aware of and alert to these signals, which will be a comfort at a hugely difficult and challenging time (said Jesus, "lift up your heads" (Luke 21: 28). Trumpets (or Shofarim) may in reality be also the time that God has marked out for His Son's return – we do not know the year or the "time", but we do definitely have some sense as to the time of year[11]. Messiah's eternal rule will begin at a defined point in time. Immediately following the commencement of His rule there will be a judgment on all those who rebelled against Him. Babylon will have fallen! Finally He will "tabernacle" (live with) His people; then God will literally dwell with Mankind in peace.

The above schema "works" assuming, also, that the millennial rule ends in rebellion as Satan is released from the Abyss for his final foray into the world (Revelation 20: 7-8). Mankind, in rebellion, and almost certainly in some way repeating his attempt to destroy the locus of God's earthly rule (Israel), reveals his determination not to live under God's rule – in spite of having lived for 1,000 years in peace, security and order. This time there will be absolutely no excuse, and judgment will be swift and definitive. Then, and only then, shall God create a New Heaven and a New Earth (Revelation 21). These are not separate entities as some suggest; in fact they are a single entity, as the two that were separate have now become eternally one. At this point the wedding of the Lamb finally takes place and God tabernacles with His chosen bride (all those who were true to Him) throughout eternity. Then it will truly be life without end, and truly that wonderful time of eternal shalom! What else can we say but 'hallelujah'!

Assuming that what we have proffered our readers here is correct, then 1,000 years separate Trumpets from Tabenacles *in our schematic above*. 2,000 years (or more?) separate Messiah's ascension (in AD 27?) and His return. If 1,000 years separate His return and the *final* judgment, then in total God's

---

10 n.b. those that remain true to Jesus *until the end* – as opposed to the apostate church (See Peter Sammons' "Rebel Church" for insights into the great apostasy) that will "go-over" progressively to side with Babylon (see David Lambourn "Babel Versus Bible" for more insight into this aspect of the End Time).

11 In our schematic there are two vertical bars signalling the start of the Jewish agricultural-farming year, being March-April by our calendar, and the start of the civic (government) year in September-October. What could be more natural that the time of Christ's government on earth should begin at the time the civic or governing year began for the ancient Jewish nation?

Salvific dealings with Mankind will have reached approximately 7,000 years in total. This is surely a reflection or echo of the week of Creation of Genesis chapter 1 and, in fact, the Bible states intriguingly "**with the Lord a day is like a thousand years, and a thousand years are like a day**" (2 Peter 3: 8). In Scripture seven is always a number of completion and of perfection; perhaps we are seeing something of this in the idea that the final 'era' of Mankind is his "sixth day" (in that sixth millennium of God's dealings with Mankind, in the sixth "day" of God's Salvation plan). The seventh "day" then becomes the era of holiness and perfection *that shall have no end*. Six in Scripture is the number of Man, and 666 the unholy trinity that opposes God[12].

Man's final opportunity for redemption must end. Redemption by *unsighted* faith (so praised and so affirmed throughout Scripture) surely must end in that 'sixth day' of Mankind's history. We believe that 'salvation' will still be possible and will still be a reality during that 'seventh day' of Messiah's rule here on earth and that Salvation will be on precisely the same terms – that is, by confession of sin, repentance for sin, and turning towards Jesus the Saviour. There is no reason to suggest baptism will not continue to be an outward marker of faith and evidence of rebirth. Even in the 'seventh day' being born again will still be the reality and the outcome of true faith. What will be different, perhaps, will be the presence here on Earth of Messiah Jesus reigning in reality, bringing righteous rule to Earth and presiding over a society that actually works in the interests of its people as directed by God the Son. In that sense (alone) the decision to follow Messiah will *not* be 'unsighted' as it is today.

What must we learn from this today? The Lamb's book of Life shall contain (indeed it contains today) the names of all those who have been redeemed. This register of the elect contains the names of those redeemed during the Last Days. There will also be included in this those saved *before* the Last Days (as we have defined it in this book), in essence those saved by faith but to whom was not given the good news of Salvation through the sacrificial blood of the Messiah. Whilst they did not live in the Last Days, they are beneficiaries of the finished work of Messiah upon the Cross. Your author readily acknowledges that this is deeply 'theological' territory and that there may be more than one way of understanding these wonderful truths.

The Bible is clear that *this* is the day of Salvation (2 Corinthians 6: 2), and that is why it is always profoundly urgent to close with God's offer of Salvation *when it is made*. Hebrews 10:26 tells us that "**if we sin willfully after we have received the knowledge of the truth, there no longer remains a sacrifice for sins**". During

---

12 See Peter Sammons "The Messiah Pattern" for a useful Appendix exploring the significance of the number seven in the Bible.

that seventh millennium all of Mankind (both men and women) will have received knowledge of the truth, and they will have lived under Christ's glorious rule – and yet some will reject even that. Ironically they shall have lived by sight rather than by faith, and yet even this first-hand knowledge of goodness is rejected[13]. So that is when the Lamb's book of life shall close forever (whilst they are alive, and not when they are dead). Your author here acknowledges that these things are difficult to understand, but can only encourage readers to work through and to pray through the implications. The millennial rule of Christ is truly "last chance saloon" for Mankind, yet *today* is the day of Salvation.

Praise God indeed!

---

13 Is there a faint recollection here of Adam and Eve, who lived *in sight* yet still rejected God's clear command?

CHAPTER 14

PRAISE GOD

**no one in heaven or on the earth or under the earth was able
to open the scroll or even look inside it.
I wept and wept because no one was found worthy to open
the scroll or look inside. Then one of the elders
said to me, "Do not weep. See the lion of the tribe of Judah,
the Root of David, has triumphed.
He is able to open the scroll and its seven seals" (Revelation 5: 3-5).**

New religions?

In this book we have sought to set out the key elements of the Last Days, and especially to focus on the End Time. We have largely avoided the stale debates of 'theologians' (whether official, or self-styled) and sought instead to revisit the words of Jesus, as it is He who has given us the clearest description of what to expect in our collective future. Jesus tells us what lies ahead, and God the Father has already declared straightforwardly that *He knows the end from the beginning* (Isaiah 46:10).

At the time of writing this book the world was emerging from a period of international enforced isolation universally known as the 'lockdown'[1] following the emergence of a new disease. It must be observed that few in the institutional churches, let alone anywhere else in the secular sphere, wondered or discussed whether this could be the outrider to 'a storm' of biblical significance. Whether what became popularised as the covid-19 'pandemic' would be associated with the end of the Last Days as we have defined it in this book, or even the beginning of the End Time, is really not the question at issue. Your author is 'agnostic' on this

---

1 A word that emerged in the USA, originally as a tactical device of police forces to cordon-off an area or a neighbourhood so as to ferret out criminals. This tactic was also associated with the USA's penchant for using paramilitary SWAT teams to conduct *search and enforcement* operations. In a lockdown all citizens were to remain in their houses or places of business until the "lock" on ordinary life was lifted, generally within a few hours. Perhaps slightly ironic that such a term was so readily applied, not to streets or neighbourhoods, but to entire nations and for months on end. Why? Because the new religion of science decreed, and the populace was duly (and often willingly) cowed.

matter, except to say that he believes that the God who Self-identifies as the God of Jacob is unquestionably on the move in our day.

As a result of the purported success of Mankind's response to the covid disease, science became *the great white hope* of the masses and was semi-deified. Scientists were lauded as 'saviours', and the TV oracles and daily pronouncements of scientists (as 'talking heads') were received, if not universally, with gratitude and relief. Meantime western governments claimed to "follow the science". In the Western world, if not more widely, the message spread amongst 'the chatterati' that "we can now cure anything" via a new active technology (mRNA technology) that had been rolled-out universally to the masses without the normal and irksome distraction of long-term testing, observation and licensing. 'Scientism' became essentially a new faith system, as mankind, by and large, placed its new found faith in 'experts'. Mankind was at last in control! Mankind was fashioning his own future in his own image and, by extension, neither needed – nor brooked – interference from a Creator God. It seemed that, on the back of the international responses to the covid-19 drama, moves towards globalised control, globalised institutions with globalised law making and tax-raising powers, and even global government, had advanced with surprisingly little comment, nor concern. From the perspective of Cultural Marxism these were indeed welcome outcomes as they simultaneously advanced the cause of social revolution. The events of 2020-21 coincided with a new political movement known as "black lives matter" and near universal Western fear (terror?) of "global climate change". 'Racial justice' and 'climate justice' became the new catch-phrases, capturing the mood and objectives of the 'chatterati'. And climate change would also, of course, be 'solved' by those new *high priests of science*. Governments everywhere would "follow the science".

The 'Christian' leaders of the institutional churches had very little of note to say on these global developments other than to adopt a 'managerial' posture, closing churches and implementing 'social distancing'[2] with a zeal often lacking in their secular counterparts, whilst publicly endorsing the broadly 'woke' agendas of the world at large. For the past fifty years, or more, large segments of the institutional churches have perceived themselves as essentially *the religious arm of the welfare state*, with no vital gospel to proclaim, or to defend. The blood of Jesus was out of fashion. God's prophetic purpose as expressed

---

2 It was perhaps emblematic of a wider malaise that at a time of social *distancing* and literally separating people from normal encounters, the institutional churches seemed happy and enthused to 'close the gap' with other religions, as interfaith-multifaith initiatives were increasingly promoted.

in Scripture was similarly an embarrassment to some parts of 'the church', especially those known as 'Liberals' who appear to believe that we live today in a golden era where mankind will progressively get better and better, as the world is progressively 'Christianised' via social enterprises. They seem to think that when the world is a nice enough place, then "Jesus" (rarely *the Lord Jesus* in their expression!) may finally return.

Despite the above, in all that we have explored so far in this book your author hopes that a rising sense of praise, hope and wonder has been engendered in the hearts of readers. Our God really is in control, and no matter how uncomfortable (or deadly) times may become for the true disciple of Yeshua, God will work out His eternal purposes. Our glorious expectation, and hope, is to tabernacle with Him through eternity.

At this point we should pause and turn our gaze once again upon the glorious gospel of the Kingdom. Sadly our world rejects this gospel, by and large. Indeed to the World the gospel remains a 'scandal' and an 'offense' (1 Corinthians 1: 23 [3]). Our world today in the early 2020s has its own totally absorbing agendas – characterised by running hither and thither, desperately (and vainly) trying to 'turn down the world's thermostat', wear black masks and hide from invisible microscopic enemies. All this, whilst trying to avoid acknowledgement of the increasing tempo of war's continuous drumbeat, ignoring social and cultural decay, and hoping (like Micawber in Charles Dickens' novel "David Copperfield") that "something will turn up". That 'something' is likely to involve the future urgent search for a worldwide 'saviour' whom the Bible calls 'antichrist'. So far, so sad – and so very predictable.

In this book we try to avoid speculation about future events. Some Christians have set themselves up as virtually full-time prophetic 'think tanks', commenting in huge detail about global events and linking these to biblical prophecy. Whilst it is certainly noble to wrestle with the Word of God (something we have sought to do in this book), we should not do this to aggrandise ourselves, or to play to a gallery of likeminded religious people, nor to promote a particular schema of Christianised futurism, or our own favoured 'systematic theology'. Where Christians address the future, we should do so with a due sense of reverence, always bearing in mind that God wisely and graciously obscured His end-time plans and distributed 'clues' about His purposes across and throughout Scripture. The truth is discernable to the diligent searcher after truth, but only after much effort, prayer and invested time. There are no 'easy' answers . . .

---

3 the translation "stumbling block" is probably too tame an expression!

Accordingly in this book we have studiously avoided detailed commentary on the place of Turkey, Russia, China, the EU and so on in End Time realities, albeit we are reasonably certain each of these actors will have their role to play. Likewise we have not commented in any detail on "the king of the north" or "the king of the south", nor even the very intriguing absence of any king of the west! Whilst these matters are inevitably of considerable interest (even of concern), we caution against investing much time and energy in pursuit of such insights, as God will undoubtedly make plain these matters to His faithful remnant, *as and when the time is right* – and not before! Rather, our task remains (as Jesus did, and as Jesus commanded) to preach the good news of the Kingdom and to make disciples of all nations (Matthew 4:23 and Matthew 28:19).

The good news is that the good news IS good news!

It must be notable that the Lord Jesus did not say that the good news is that you can be forgiven of your sins, or avoid Hell, or even that you can 'go to heaven' when you die. No, He taught simply that *the good news is the news of the Kingdom*, that is, the place where God's righteous and loving rule is experienced both today and into eternity, and how near it is. In the UK for many years there was a television comedy series called "One Foot in the Grave" about a hapless recent retiree constantly trying to find a new role and a new purpose in life, and never quite succeeding. For the believer we have 'one foot in eternity' as soon as we have come to Jesus and received Him as our Lord and as Saviour. Yes, of course we have one foot in this world as we continue to live out our lives here. But we do so as citizens[4] of The Kingdom, where our true loyalty now lies. So we have one foot in eternity right now, with the guarantee of "tabernacling" with Yeshua throughout eternity. That is His promise to us, and it is our great objective . . . to be with Him.

How then can we 'define' God's purpose in Messiah Yeshua? It has been said that t*he story of salvation is like a red cord that runs throughout Scripture*, from Genesis to Revelation. That is surely an apt simile, as the red cord reminds us of the blood of our Saviour, shed for us. And we know that Yeshua was sacrificed for us, *from the foundation of the world* (Revelation 13: 8). In other words, it was always the plan of the Father and the Son, that the Son would give Himself up for Mankind. This red cord is discernable both directly and indirectly throughout the Old Testament (as we shall see shortly) especially in "types"

---

4 Perhaps that more correctly should be "subjects of the Kingdom"! as we have a King and we are His subjects! The Kingdom is not a democracy, nor is it a republic! We are eternal subjects to our eternal King.

and "shadows" that pepper the Scriptures. We repeat, it was always the plan of the Father and the Son, that the Son would give Himself for Mankind. Praise God! Praise Jesus! How then can we summarise what has been done, what has been achieved? In the next few pages, using the **International Standard Version** (except one reference taken from the **Christian Standard Bible**), we allow the Bible itself to comment upon the attitude of God towards Mankind. The emphases in bold type are added by the editors here, but we hope they adequately display the 'love aforethought' of God the Saviour:

God's Word in Scripture

The Lord is not slow about his promise, as some people understand slowness, but is being patient with you. **He does not want anyone to perish**, but everyone to find room for **repentance**.

2 Peter 3:9

AUTHOR COMMENT:

God is reluctant to judge and condemn. Of course ultimately He must do so, but it is not His primary purpose. His primary purpose is to build a family of those who joyfully receive His Son as Lord. Amongst this true family, God will "tabernacle" forever.

It is the Lord's 'strange work' (Isaiah 28:21) to judge. History testifies that judgment is something God is reluctant to do. Consider all the wickedness that has marred human history, all the sin and disregard for God and for His laws. Think of how few times He has intervened with judgment. Through the prophet Ezekiel, God said, "I have no pleasure in the death of the wicked" (33:11). Truly, God is reluctant to judge.

God delights in showing mercy (Micah 7:18). Israel's rebellious history reveals that its people were often on the brink of extinction because of their sin. The book of Judges, for example, covers an approximately 335-year period of great moral confusion when "everyone did what was right in his own eyes" (Judges 17:6). Perhaps that sounds like our world today!

So God does not "tarry". He is giving time for as many to be saved as possible. *This is the day of salvation*. This is the harvesting season! But the harvesting season will reach its end, eventually.

God's Word in Scripture

This is good and acceptable in the sight of God our Saviour, **who wants all people to be saved** and to come to know the truth fully. There is one God. There is also one mediator between God and human beings – a human, the Messiah Jesus. He **gave himself as a ransom for everyone**, the testimony at the proper time.

1 Timothy 2: 3-6

AUTHOR COMMENT:

We repeat, it is God's great purpose that all should be saved. Not all will be saved, tragically. Ultimately rejection of Yeshua is the conscious and determined choice of the Christ-rejector. Yet . . .

Yeshua gave Himself, willingly, for all. The purpose of Jesus in coming to this world could not be clearer.

God's Word in Scripture

No man can redeem the life of another, nor can he give to God a sufficient payment for him. For it would cost too much to redeem his life, and the **payments would go on forever -** that he should go on living and not see corruption.

Psalm 49: 7-9

AUTHOR COMMENT:

We cannot earn our "salvation" in any way, shape or form[5]. We need to repent of our good deeds just as much as our bad deeds! We tend to put our faith in our response to God's open hand of forgiveness. We think we can 'earn' a little bit of our salvation, but we cannot!

The point here is painfully clear: we cannot afford the debt, so Yeshua steps in and pays it for us. We cannot possibly go on paying forever and ever. No, our debt is settled on the Cross; our only righteous response is to receive Yeshua and accept in faith, His death in place of ours.

Psalm 49: 7-9 is given as a "signpost" to Jesus.

---

5 This rather puts paid to the philosophy of 'universalism' wherein an indeterminate period of time spent in purgatory (punishment) results in salvation. Psalm 49 verse 8 makes it clear that *no payment* is *ever* enough (NIV translation). By contrast the sacrifice of Jesus is enough - so we conclude that this is the day of salvation.

God's Word in Scripture

He was wounded for our transgressions, and he was crushed for our iniquities, and the punishment that made us whole was upon him, and by his bruises we are healed. All we like sheep have gone astray, we have turned, each of us, to his own way; **and the Lord has laid on him the iniquity of us all**. He was oppressed and he was afflicted, yet he didn't open his mouth; like a lamb that is led to the slaughter, as a sheep that before its shearers is silent, so he did not open his mouth.

Isaiah 53: 5-7

AUTHOR COMMENT:

Upon Yeshua has been placed our "iniquity", that is, our sins and our rebellions.

Jesus gave no word in His Own defence. God knows He could have done! But at the day of judgment, He will give a word in *our* defence. And that word will be final and definitive.

Isaiah 53: 5-7 is given as a "signpost" to Jesus.

God's Word in Scripture

For I passed on to you the most important points that I received: **the Messiah died for our sins according to the Scriptures**, he was buried, he was raised on the third day according to the Scriptures—and is still alive!—

1 Corinthians 15: 3-4

AUTHOR COMMENT:

It is a simple record of history: Yeshua died on the cross. *And He died for us, not for Himself.*

But He arose from the grave, and that is our eternal guarantee that the task is complete, the job is finished. Finished once. Finished for all who will receive Him.

Notice, incidentally, that Jesus died for our sins *according to the Scriptures* – that is, according to the Old Testament! This should be a wake-up call to those "Christians" who say the Old Testament is now redundant!

God's Word in Scripture

For God loved the world in this way: He gave His one and only Son, so that **everyone who believes in Him will not perish but have eternal life**

John 3:16 (CSB)

AUTHOR COMMENT:

Yes, God has demonstrated His love for us in this, that whilst we were still sinners, Messiah died for us (Romans 5:8).

It is tough love, and it cost Jesus everything. It cost the Father His one and only Son. How much more can God demonstrate His love?

Most modern Bible translations ("God so loved" or even "God loved the world so much") have rather got this wrong. In seventeenth-century English "God so loved the world" was in fact correct. This phrase is quite right in the old King James Bible. But in today's language it would be better rendered "God thus loved the world" which then (obviously) refers back to John 3:14, which is the kernel of the gospel. Look it up!

God's Word in Scripture

Truly, I tell all of you emphatically, whoever hears what I say and believes in the one who sent me **has eternal life** and will not be judged, but has **passed from death to life**.

John 5:24

AUTHOR COMMENT:

The matter is settled! Praise God!

Those who believe on Jesus are saved eternally. We will stand before the judgment seat. We shall be publicly "judged". Yet we will be acquitted not because of lack of evidence, or on account of our supposed "good works", but because Yeshua says, in effect, "this debt has already been paid. It was paid on the nail, by Me".

God's Word in Scripture

They answered, "**Believe** on the Lord Jesus, and **you** and your family **will be saved**."

Acts 16:31

AUTHOR COMMENT:

This translation is better than some others! We are not called to believe "in", but to believe "on". There is a vast difference. We encourage readers to explore the implications.

Oh yes! The good news is that the good news IS good news! It is not that bad news to which this World tries to traduce it. As we consider these great truths, we can but rejoice and praise God for His wisdom and His great mercy. In the words of the apostle Paul in Romans 11: 33-36:

Oh, the depth of the riches of the wisdom and knowledge of God!
How unsearchable his judgments,
and his paths beyond tracing out!
"Who has known the mind of the Lord?
Or who has been his counsellor?"
"Who has ever given to God,
 that God should repay them?"
For from him and through him and for him are all things.
To him be the glory forever! Amen. (NIV)

That surely has to be our response as we begin to engage with the awesome truth that God determined His plan of salvation from the beginning, and graciously prefigured it to the eyes of faith. We have only to open our eyes to see!

The Last Days and End Time

As we explored earlier in this book, the days in which we live today are the last days, in terms of God's salvific dealings with Mankind. The Last Days extend from the ascension until Jesus returns in glory.

Two points emerge straightway – *this is the day of salvation* (not tomorrow) and Salvation as a remedy and as a reality will persist into the millennial rule of Messiah Jesus.

God does not extend the opportunity of 'salvation' beyond this world. That is why the Catholic 'theology' of *purgatory* must be pronounced false. God is drawing to Himself *today* a willing and loving family, of those who have determinedly chosen Him in this life, and have taken up their cross daily and followed Him, not been bullied-into it through some other supposed future existence. The 'cross hairs' of all Scripture is focused on these Last Days, and that surely is the whole point of Creation.

Those who refuse God because they want to be 'god' over their own lives will ultimately achieve their purpose, but in the process they only become 'god' over their regrets and sorrows at having ignored so great a Salvation (Hebrews 2: 3). That loss persists beyond the grave. Some would fearfully argue that this is somehow not 'loving' on the part of God; that is a question far too broad for us to tackle here [6]. And it is a question that, even were it to be answered fully, a perverse, foolish and finite human cannot really understand the explanation, in any case. It is sheer hubris to pretend that we can [7]. However we can at least posit this as a partial answer: God's 'love' (hesed, agape) is displayed in separating eternally the sheep from the goats, as in so doing He makes evident and real His vindication of all those who have suffered persecution so grievously for the past two millennia and shows them that His "husbandry" of them was - and is - perfection. Justice will prevail. Those *justified* by Jesus go to be with Him eternally in a loving and willing and joyful family.

As Jesus will rule in His millennial Kingdom and as aging and death shall continue during that period, we understand that Salvation for eternity will still be offered and still given on precisely the same basis, that is, upon the finished work of Jesus through the cross of crucifixion. Praise God indeed! Whilst in some senses it may be 'easier' for humans during the millennial rule to see the truthfulness of the Messiah's claim, yet even then we have the sense that some will resist his call of love and righteousness, and will still actively reject Him. How tragic! But all this displays and parades once again the wisdom, righteousness and love of God *in practical action* – during the millennial rule He will continue to save the penitent sinner.

We have said little about what some call The Great Tribulation. Certainly we have not made it a separate subject in its own right. However we alluded to it in chapters 5, 6 and 9. **The Baker Encyclopedia of the Bible** (page 2105) contains a brilliant exploration of the whole subject of tribulation across Scripture in both Old and New Testaments, and we do not wish to revisit what others have so ably exposed and taught. We would simply summarise that the period immediately preceding Messiah's return will be one of unprecedented "troubles" for Mankind, giving humans the final opportunity to come to Jesus on Jesus' terms. It is rightly said that the tribulation leading to the fall of Jerusalem in AD70 is a "type" of the trouble yet to come in our common future. Within this final "big trouble" (in the words of Bible expositor David Pawson) will also come *the time of Jacob's trouble*. That will be a time when the world's attention will be focused on Israel (Jacob) as it tries to impose its agenda on to God's ancient people living in God's ancient land. Jacob's trouble will

---

6 John Benton's book "How Can a God of Love Send People to Hell" may be a helpful exploration for those who are troubled by, or fearful of, the implications of what we are expressing here.

7 It is argued by UK writer Steve Maltz that such "reasoning" represents the application of a "Greek" mind to what is essentially an "Hebraic" revelation. See Steve Maltz "Hebraic Church". This Greek mind finds it hugely difficult to adequately engage with God's revelation – it struggles incessantly.

simultaneously usher in the end of the End Times. What comes next will be the millennial rule of Messiah Jesus.

Beware the "prophets"!

We have not sought to name dates and times. It is up to readers to form their own opinions about what Scripture reveals and Jesus has said, specifically. In Appendices 1 to 4 readers can make their own assessment as to the dashboard of history; which signals are glowing green, which amber and which red? When readers see a majority of signals persisting in red then, in the words of Yeshua, we must "lift up our heads" because we shall know that our "time of redemption draws near" (Luke 21:28). Praise God!

One firm opinion we have developed as we have looked into this matter is that the return of the Lord will be at either the Hebrew feast of Trumpets or at the Hebrew feast of Tabernacles, both being autumn feasts! But we certainly do not know the year. We would not debate with anyone who holds a different view – that is their privilege! At one level the timing is less important than the fact – *our Lord is on His way*. He will return to this world at the time of the Father's choosing. Praise God again! God is in absolute control.

Any reader who has reached this point in the book is likely to be aware of, and we hope sensitive to, false teachers and false teaching. However, for the record we would urge: *do not be "led" by so-called prophets, especially if they have a financial interest in your support of their "ministry"*. Yes, there are prophets today, or perhaps we should say, those with the gift of prophetic insight. Good Bible teachers should indeed be sought out – they can genuinely help us to understand and to prepare. But modern "prophets" who failed to see the 2020 Coronavirus coming, are unlikely to be able to specify times, seasons and dates. Jesus has already done so, in any case! It is He to Whom ultimately we should look in expectancy. It is to Him, and only to Him, Whom we should listen.

We have avoided too much speculation about the present woes and difficulties of mankind. They are all interesting and possibly even relevant. We think of "spermageddon" [8], of the collapse of biodiversity, of climate change, of the rise of new global powers and the decline of old ones. And then there is the whole area of gender dysphoria wherein Mankind seeks to overturn God's Creation ordinance as given in Genesis chapter 2. All these things surely are 'shofar blasts', warning us ahead of time. And yet we must note that such difficulties have periodically manifested themselves in the history of

---

8 Another reason why the Bible posits no "King of the West"?

humankind (except perhaps the modern 'gender' wars, and associated 'identity politics') and have often been mistaken for signs of imminent collapse. Jesus calls us to be watchful and faithful. Those who are watchful will recognise the signs of the times. Those who are not . . . well, Matthew 25: 1-13 gives us a clear insight.

As regards the whole gender miasma we offer only one prophetic insight: a modern author (Yuval Harari) posits the idea that Mankind must take responsibility for his own development, and presumably work out his own 'salvation' thereby. We confess we have not read his book! Through ongoing self-development Mankind will be Homo Deus – man as god – which is the title of Harari's book. Certainly we perceive this same idea as, increasingly, hubristic Mankind believes he can do anything and now even seeks out 'the elixir of life'. But in terms of how 'Mankind' is developing your author sees a 'progression' of ideas from the mid-1960s, to today, and then on into the future. It is the gender miasma that seems to be the engine (or catalyst) for these 'developments' within Man's collective imaginings:

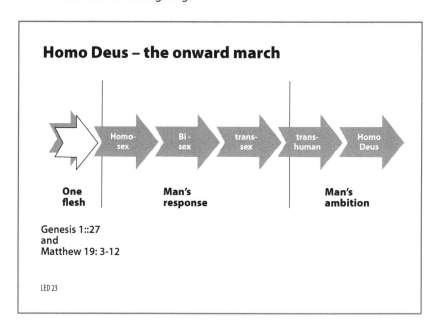

Homo Deus – the onward march

Homo-sex · Bi-sex · trans-sex · trans-human · Homo Deus

One flesh — Man's response — Man's ambition

Genesis 1::27
and
Matthew 19: 3-12

LED 23

Each of the terms used above is in the daily lexicon of today's 'chatterati', so we shall not comment on them at all. Readers can undertake their own private research if they are so minded. But the trajectory here seems plain, and the clear objective is to distance Mankind permanently from God's specific Creation ordinance, given in Genesis chapter 1 and repeated by the Lord Jesus in Matthew chapter 19. Using Britain as a sort of exemplar of Western social 'progress' underway (or is it social regress?), we can posit these thoughts: in 1967 huge legal changes were made under the then Labour government and its Home Secretary Roy Jenkins. Two key legislative Acts related to decriminalisation of homosexual activity and the legalisation of abortion. Abortion would be tightly controlled, the progressives assured people in the 1960s. Today in 2022 we have, essentially, abortion-on-demand for any reason whatsoever. So the British determined they were 'godlike' enough to kill the unborn in the mother's womb. They were going to control life's 'checking-in' and make this convenient to the 'parents' – if not to the unborn baby. At the time of writing this book there are calls for the legalisation of euthanasia under the innocuous sounding title of "assisted suicide", which of course will, we have been assured, be tightly controlled. So now Mankind claims it can control the 'checking-out' process as well.

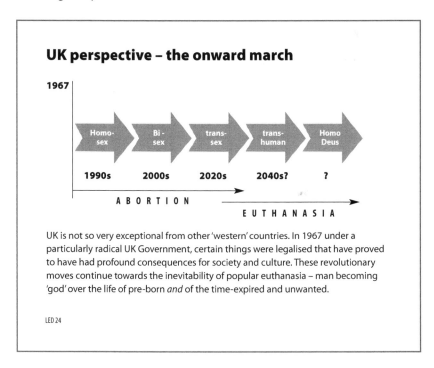

UK perspective – the onward march

UK is not so very exceptional from other 'western' countries. In 1967 under a particularly radical UK Government, certain things were legalised that have proved to have had profound consequences for society and culture. These revolutionary moves continue towards the inevitability of popular euthanasia – man becoming 'god' over the life of pre-born *and* of the time-expired and unwanted.

LED 24

This "onward march" of progress suggests that life is becoming increasingly cheap, even in supposedly 'civilised' Britain. We know full well that any 'safeguards' will be widely abused once the 'checking-out' process is licensed to private conversations between 'doctors' (or 'mentors') and the desperate or the bullied patient, nearing life's end. So if we control life before birth and at its end, then have we elevated ourselves to mini deities? Is 'Homo Deus' becoming social and philosophical fact? The UK's institutional churches were deafeningly silent on these matters in the early 2020s. Beware the secular/atheist prophets, as much as the religious ones!

That the institutional 'churches' will be thoroughly apostate (in rebellion against the Holy Spirit) when Yeshua returns, is a given [9]. Today we find an institutional 'church' that is aligned increasingly to the World's agendas in a vain endeavor to seem 'relevant'. At the time of writing this book, climate change had become the institutional church's new lodestar, whilst the current Pope effectively pronounced that all religions are one [10]. By any historical yardstick it is difficult to call Pope Francis a Catholic, but in a world where "anything goes", for a Pope to redefine Catholicism in his own image is perhaps hardly surprising.

Whilst we urge our readers to beware of certain "prophets" we can but commend to everyone Him who is eternally Prophet, Priest and King – Yeshua ha Massiasch, Jesus the Messiah. He who is the true forth-teller of God's purposes (that's what a genuine prophet does, and Jesus is *the anointed* Prophet) provides clarity for us as to what to expect in the future. He has already displayed His credentials by predicting His Own resurrection from death. It is He who is the ultimate High Priest, and a priest in the order of Melchizedek. Jesus is the High Priest who shall preside forever. It is He who is the final King of Israel, of the line of David and reigning on His Father's throne forever. Interesting, informative and even urgent though the study of the End Times may be, the most vital task of all peoples everywhere is simple: it is to respond to Jesus either in faith and acceptance, or in doubt and rejection. The Last Days have persisted since Pentecost. How much longer will they continue?

Praise God indeed.

---

9 Peter Sammons' book "Rebel Church" was freely available as a PDF at the time this book was prepared.

10 "Is the Pope a Catholic?": https://christiancomment.org/2021/06/16/interfaithism-2/

APPENDICES

Appendices 1 – 4 : EXPLANATORY NOTE

Appendices 1 to 4 depict many prophetic streams/themes related to the End Time but we cluster them under four key headings:

- World Events • Israel • Moral Decay • The Gospel

These prophetic streams overlap and some references given are repeated in more than one stream.

We depict all this information as a set of 'warning lights', as if on an instrument panel or dashboard. The warning signs can be understood as through the idea of a traffic light (red, amber, green). Our 'RAG dashboards' (red, amber, green) relate to Chapters 4 and 7.

Readers are encouraged to consider for themselves what 'status' our present world may have reached in terms of whether these prophetic signs presently stand at 'red', or 'amber' or 'green'. This is certainly not 'an exact science' and different readers will have differing views and insights. But Jesus Himself warned, and Scripture generally indicates, clear observational signs to help us identify the nearness of the Lord's return. Jesus described them as "birth pangs" (Matthew 24: 8).

We must note that, throughout history, virtually all of these signs have periodically emerged (moved, as it were, from 'green' into 'red') and have appeared imminent ('red') only later to return to 'amber' and then to 'green'. They have waxed and waned. It is not the individual signs but rather the coincidence of all these signs, and their eventual urgent persistence (remaining at 'red') that will give confidence that we are approaching the End Time. We can therefore think of these signs collectively as constituting a "dashboard" that informs us of the bigger picture.

Whilst the Bible does not include specific prophecies regarding abortion, euthanasia or child abuse as signs of the end time, it does refer repeatedly to a widespread, near universal, rejection of (and indeed rebellion against) God's values as expressed in the Jewish Torah and in Jesus' own teachings. Societal endorsement of the deliberate taking of human life, whether of the very young or elderly, is a defining characteristic of our present age and as such, we believe this clearly indicates that we are approaching the climax to the Last Days as we have defined it in this book.

Readers must ultimately ponder, research and pray-into these questions to reach their own conclusion. Appendices 1 to 4 are offered as a framework within which to explore further.

World Events   *Appendix 1*

1. **'Natural' Phenomena** ○
2. **Globalisation** ○
3. **Nation Against Nation** ○
4. **Disease** ○
5. **Drought/Famine** ○
6. **Signs in the stars** ○
7. **Tribulation** ○
8. **International government** ○

1. Mark 13: 8 ■ Matt 24: 7
   Luke 21: 25–26 ■ Zech 14: 4–5

2. Rev 13: 16–18 ■ Rev 17: 18
   Psalm 2: 1–3

3. Matt 24: 6–7 and 21–22
   Mark 13: 7–8 ■ Luke 21: 9 –10

4. Matt 24: 7–8
   Luke 21:11

5. Matt 24: 6–7 (famine)
   Mark 13: 8 (famine)
   Revelation 16: 7 (drought)

6. Luke 21: 25 –26 ■ Matt 24: 29
   Mark 13: 24 –25
   Revelation 6:13 –14

7. Matt 24: 21-22 and Daniel 12:1

8. Revelation 13:1 –12

Israel

Appendix 2

1. World rises up against Israel ◯

Luke 21: 7 ■ Luke 21: 20 – 22
Past, future or both?

Isaiah 52: 7–10
Zechariah 12: 2 – 3
Zechariah 14: 1 – 4
Joel 3: 2 ■ Daniel 12:1
Revelation 9:14–16, 16:12–16

2. False peace ◯

Daniel 9: 27

3. One New Man ◯

Ephesians 2: 14

Moral Decay

Appendix 3

1. Moral Decay ⭕
Daniel 12:10 ■ Revelation 17: 2
1 Peter 2: 11–12 ■ 2 Tim 3: 1–4

2. Abortion ⭕
Psalm 139:13 –16 ■ Job 10:8–12
Jeremiah 20:17 ■ Ecclesiastes 11:5
Leviticus 20: 2–5 ■ Jeremiah 32: 35
Acts 17: 25 ■ Jeremiah 1: 5
Galatians 1: 15 ■ Luke 1: 15

3. Euthanasia ⭕
Exodus 20: 13 ■ Exodus 23: 7
2 Kings 21: 16 ■ Psalm 106: 37–8

4. Disobedience to parents ⭕
2 Timothy 3: 1–5

5. Pride ⭕
Matt 24: 6–7 ■ 2 Timothy 3: 1–5

6. Assault upon Children ⭕
Matthew 18: 5–6

7. Holy Spirit fall afresh on all Believers ⭕
Joel 2: 28 –32 ■ Matthew 10: 19–20

8. Scoffers ⭕
2 Peter 3: 3 – 4

The Gospel

Appendix 4

1. **Resistance to the Gospel** ○
   Matt 24:9 ■ Mark 13:9–11
   Luke 21:12–15

2. **Persecution of Believers** ○
   Revelation 6:9–11
   Revelation 17:6 ■ Matt 24:9
   Mark 13:9-11
   Luke 21:12–15

3. **False 'prophets'** ○
   Matt 24:24 ■ 2 Timothy 4:3–4
   2 Thessalonians 2:1–3

4. **Antichrist/Beast** ○
   Revelation 13:15
   Matthew 24:15–24
   Mark 13:14–22
   2 Thessalonians 2:1–4
   1 John 2:18 ■ Revelation 13:1–8

5. **Rebel 'church'** ○
   Revelation 17 ■ 2 Timothy 3:4
   2 Timothy 4:3–4 ■ Daniel 12:10

6. **Gospel preached across planet Earth** ○
   Matthew 24:14 ■ Mark 13:10
   Joel 2:28–32 ■ Acts 2:14–21

7. **New world religion** ○
   Revelation 13:all
   Revelation 17 (?)

8. **Increase of Knowledge** ○
   (by believers of spiritual situation)
   Daniel 12:4 ■ Matthew 24:all
   Mark 13:all ■ Luke 21:5–36

Appendix 5

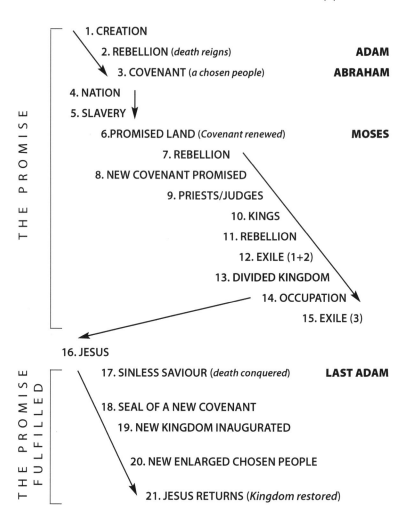

THE PROMISE

1. CREATION
2. REBELLION (*death reigns*)   **ADAM**
3. COVENANT (*a chosen people*)   **ABRAHAM**
4. NATION
5. SLAVERY
6. PROMISED LAND (*Covenant renewed*)   **MOSES**
7. REBELLION
8. NEW COVENANT PROMISED
9. PRIESTS/JUDGES
10. KINGS
11. REBELLION
12. EXILE (1+2)
13. DIVIDED KINGDOM
14. OCCUPATION
15. EXILE (3)

16. JESUS

THE PROMISE FULFILLED

17. SINLESS SAVIOUR (*death conquered*)   **LAST ADAM**
18. SEAL OF A NEW COVENANT
19. NEW KINGDOM INAUGURATED
20. NEW ENLARGED CHOSEN PEOPLE
21. JESUS RETURNS (*Kingdom restored*)

A note on the biblical references:
These references are the author's personal selection. Many others might have been selected to illustrate the same points, but hopefully these contain sufficient directness and precision to emphasize the broad roadmap of Salvation History.

Appendix 5a

1. Genesis 1-2; Ps 33: 6-9; Isa 50: 2-3; Job 38: 1-18

2. Genesis 3

3. Gen 12:1–9; Gen 15:1–21; Gen 17:1–14

4. Gen 12:2–3; Ps 33:12

5. Ex 1–12 inclusive

6. Josh 1:1–9; 12 inclusive; 13:1–7; Ps 105:6; Isa 41:9

7. Throughout Old Testament (Tanakh)

8. Jeremiah 31:31–33; Deut 29:4; Exek 36: 26-27; Jeremiah 31:31-33; Hebrews 8: 6-13

9. Judges 1-21 inclusive / 1 Samuel 1–7 inclusive

10. 1 Samuel 8 inclusive; 1 Sam 16:1–13; 1 and 2 Kings inclusive; 2 Chronicles 36:5–8

11. 1 and 2 Kings inclusive

12. 2 Chronicles 36:13–23; [Babylonian 1] Jeremiah 52:1–34 [Babylonian 2]

13. 2 Chronicles 10:1–19

14. Roman occupation is not explained in Scripture, although there are allusions to it.

15. Exile under Rome is not recorded in Scripture. Exile alluded to by Jesus in Matthew 24 Revelation 16:1-7 may prefigure the Roman exile.

16. Matthew, Mark, Luke, John (Gospels) inclusive

17. 1 John 2:2; 1 John 1:5–7; Coloss 2:9–15; Philippians 2:6–11; Coloss 1:15–23
    SECOND ADAM (1 Cor 15:45)

18. Matt 26:26–30; Luke 22:17–20; 1 Cor 11:23–25; Rev 5:6–14

19. Matt 6:33; Matt 12:28; Luke 11:20; Matt 8:11; Acts 1:6–8.
    There are several levels of meaning to 'Kingdom

20. Romans 9–11 inclusive; Romans 11:11–24 especially; Galatians 3:26–29;
    Ephesians 4:4–5; Rev 7:8–10; Rev 14:6–7

21. Rev 19:1–9; Rev 21:1–7; Rev 22:7–17; Acts 1:11

A note on the periods of exile:
Deportation of defeated enemy leaders was a common feature of both Assyrian and Babylonian empires. In the Bible the term 'the exile' or 'captivity' refers to the deportation of Judah's leaders from Jerusalem in the 6th century BC. Earlier, the leaders of the Northern Kingdom (Israel) had been deported by the Assyrians, following the fall of Samaria in 722 BC.

Appendix 6 – Multiple Fulfilments of Prophecy

Precisely When?

Prophecy in the Bible very often has a near- term and a long- term, or dual- aspect, outworking. Near-term would have resonated with people at the time the prophecy was given. Long-term would be fulfilled later – and some fulfilments remain as yet in our collective future, even today. Some of the prophecies of Jesus' birth are clear examples of near- and far- term outworking. Much prophecy seems to incorporate this duality.

Jewish people refer to the Hebrew Scriptures ("Old Testament") as the Tanakh, a word based on the first letter of each of the three types of literature which comprise it – the Torah ("the Law"), the Nevi'im ("the prophets"), and the Ketuvim ("the writings"). It is in the Tanakh that we find most prophetic utterance as God communicates with His *Chosen People*.

The New Testament also contains a significant amount of prophecy, the substantial majority of which expands on passages from the Tanakh, particularly those in Ezekiel, Jeremiah, Zechariah, Daniel and Isaiah. It is estimated that the book of Revelation has around 300 references or allusions to the Tanakh prophets, so attempting to fully understand Revelation without this essential Scriptural background will be challenging! This may explain why it is not uncommon to hear sermon series on Revelation which include the first few chapters (on the historical New Testament churches), but which then jump directly to the end of the book, describing Jesus' glorious and future reign. The middle section is omitted as many preachers are not especially familiar with the prophetic Tanakh background.

Jesus considered the Tanakh of supreme importance: when asked by His disciples about the timing and circumstances of His return and the end of the present age, Yeshua referred them to the prophecies written in the Book of Daniel – "**let the reader understand**" (Matthew 24:15). The passage in question concerns the "**abomination that causes desolation**", and describes the desecration of the Jewish temple in Jerusalem. The disciples would immediately have recalled an event from their relatively recent history, when the powerful foreign ruler Antiochus Epiphanes had slaughtered a pig on the Jerusalem temple altar and erected a statue of Zeus in the Holy of Holies, with his own face engraved on it. Furthermore, they would have recognised these events (as indeed do most serious modern theologians), as fulfilment of Daniel's prophecy. Yet now the disiples hear Yeshua telling them that something similar will happen again in the future, and it will be one of the most significant indicators of His imminent return.

Whilst Yeshua's disciples would evidently have 'got the point', Believers today are wont to divide into different, sometimes warring, factions when it comes to interpreting His message. Why might this be? And what principles can we suggest for approaching Scripture in ways that help us navigate the confusion arising from numerous competing theologians and self-styled prophecy 'experts'?

Preconceptions

Our starting point, it is suggested, should be to consider with what preconceptions we might ourselves subconsciously, or even consciously, approach the Scripture. After all, things do look very different when wearing 'literal sun glasses', or indeed proverbial 'rose-tinted' glasses. And therein lies our first challenge; should we interpret the Bible in general, and prophecy in particular, in a literal or in a spiritual sense? In principle the answer to this question should be straightforward. After all, it is estimated that around 300 Tanakh prophecies were literally fulfilled by the Lord at His first coming, and that over 80% of Bible prophecy as a whole has likewise already demonstrably happened in recorded history. No-one would argue that Biblical prophecy concerning the destruction of Jerusalem and the respective exiles of the tribes of Israel and then Judah should be interpreted "spiritually". Why then should we therefore suddenly change our interpretative paradigm?

Some Bible students "spiritualise" prophecy because they find so many examples of the New Testament itself interpreting literal and historical events in the Tanakh as types and shadows. For example, Messiah's atoning death is foreshadowed by the Passover, whilst the Jewish exodus, wilderness and possession of the Promised Land all have much to teach Believers of every generation (1 Corinthians 10:1-13). However - and this is a distinction of vital importance - whenever the New Testament refers to as yet unfulfilled Tanakh prophecies, it continues to treat them as future, literal events, sometimes elaborating on the specific details, as Jesus Himself did when referring to the prophet Daniel. When it comes to Revelation, though, some argue that it's extraordinarily dramatic symbolism means that it should be interpreted in a *purely* spiritual sense. Whilst this view may have some merit, it overlooks the fact that Revelation uses the same imagery as the Tanakh. For example, its fearsome beasts are drawn directly from Daniel, where the literal interpretation of the symbolism is interpreted for us.

Given a tendency of some theologians to regard the New Testament as justifying a change in approach to the interpretation of prophecy, it may seem remarkable that when it comes to Messiah's prediction concerning a future desolation of the temple, everyone seems to agree that this should be understood literally. However, the tendency becomes clear when we understand that a great many teachers believe that literal Bible prophecy came to an end with the destruction of Jerusalem in AD 70, and that thereafter any as yet unfulfilled prophecy should be interpreted "spiritually". This perspective of Replacement Theology is, we would argue, a distorting and misleading lens through which to view Scripture. It fails to take into account the fact that whilst some of the details Yeshua gave us in the Olivet Discourse have historically taken place, others are yet future. Similarly, prophetic passages such as Zechariah's description of a Jewish controlled Jerusalem being a huge flash point for international conflict are surely inexplicable unless interpreted as literal and closely linked to the circumstances of the Lord's Second Coming! (The last few pages of chapter 4 are worth reviewing for readers unconvinced on this matter.)

The fact that Daniel's prophecy appears to refer to at least three separate events (at the time of the Maccabees, the Roman invasion, and a yet future scenario) - all broadly similar in nature – surely illustrates the principle that many Biblical prophecies have dual or even multiple fulfilments. Various other examples could be cited. However, the important lesson for us to realise is that some of the heated arguments between "experts" about whether "this (event) is that (prophetic fulfilment)", with those on opposing sides trying to prove each other wrong, may be entirely misplaced. There is room for both perspectives to be true, yet each being part of a much bigger picture. This matter highlights another interpretive pair of glasses that can distort our understanding of Scripture – approaching God's Word through the lens of the Greek (or Western) mindset.

Jewish or Greek?

A Biblically authentic Jewish approach to Scripture differs in many ways from how Western believers typically engage with the Bible. Although we do not have space to explore this theme in detail here, we do commend authors Steve Maltz and Jacob Prasch in particular for those who are willing to allow the Lord to challenge unhelpful preconceptions. Suffice it to draw a simple contrast to make the point. The Western mindset is to approach Scripture as an intellectual puzzle, in which a particular passage can only ever be interpreted in one "correct" way. The "Hebraic" approach is that the Word of God should lead us to worship the Lord in "spirit and in truth" in a way which increasingly transforms us into His likeness, and that Scripture presents many shades of meaning, both literal *and* spiritual, but complementing each other. Understanding the reality of multiple prophetic fulfilments is therefore easier, we would suggest, for those who seek to embrace the Hebraic mindset. We caution, however, against assuming that all Jewish methods of interpreting Scripture are valid or helpful. We entirely discount mysticism, such as the Kabbala, for example.

Most Jews also part company with Believers, of course, concerning the person of Messiah Yeshua. Here too, understanding the principle of dual or multiple fulfilment of prophecy could help to break down long-standing barriers. A classic example is Isaiah's prophecy concerning the Virgin Birth with its fulfilment at our Lord's first coming, but this prophecy also had a more immediate historical fulfilment concerning another righteous man born to a young woman. The Hebrew word "alma" being applicable to both events. Regarding this division between Jew and Gentile, Paul writes passionately about Messiah tearing down the "wall of hostility" through His death (Ephesians 2: 14), and about a future time of national repentance towards Yeshua (Romans 11: 25-26). The question for Believers (one addressed comprehensively in the book "Ruth – a Prophetic Parable" (Simon Pease, CPI, 2020)), is what part *we* might play today in helping God's ancient *Covenant People* on this journey of realisation. Will we still be in this world during the Great Tribulation to point them, and others, towards the Messiah, or will we have already departed planet Earth? We mention this simply to reiterate that Dispensationalism is another lens through which to view Scripture, and readers should be aware of this fact, regardless of their position on it.

As a final reflection on the matter of Scripture often having multiple shades (or levels) of meaning, let us bear in mind that Bible prophecy also contains vivid imagery and rich symbolism. Beasts and mountains often represent empires or kingdoms, seas can refer to peoples or to chaos, and so on. If there is one key lesson for us to learn in all these things, it must surely be to approach the Word of God with great humility. We should actively seek to allow the Holy Spirit to be its first, and its last, interpreter (John 16: 13 and 1 Corinthians 2: 10-13).

Appendix 7 – Charles Wesley – Almighty God of Love

ALMIGHTY God of love,
Set up the attracting sign,
And summon whom thou dost approve
For messengers divine;
From favoured Abraham's seed
The new apostles choose,
In isles and continents to spread
The dead-reviving news.

Them, snatched out of the flame,
Through every nation send,
The true Messiah to proclaim,
The universal friend;
That all the God unknown
May learn of Jews to adore,
And see thy glory in thy Son,
Till time shall be no more.

O that the chosen band
Might now their brethren bring,
And, gathered out of every land,
Present to Zion's King!
Of all the ancient race
Not one be left behind,
But each, impelled by secret grace,
His way to Canaan find.

We know it must be done,
For God hath spoke the word:
All Israel shall the Saviour own,
To their first state restored;
Rebuilt by his command,
Jerusalem shall rise;
Her temple on Moriah stand
Again, and touch the skies.

Send then thy servants forth,
To call the Hebrews home;
From East, and West, and South, and North,
Let all the wanderers come;
Where'er in lands unknown
The fugitives remain,
Bid every creature help them on,
Thy holy mount to gain.

An offering to their God,
There let them all be seen,
Sprinkled with water and with blood,
In soul and body clean;
With Israel's myriads sealed,
Let all the nations meet,
And show the mystery fulfilled,
Thy family complete!

Old Wesley Hymnbook – October 1799 – Ezekiel 11: 17.
Today sung to the tune: 'Crown Him with Many Crowns'.

FURTHER READING

Select list of books on the general theme of Israel

David Pawson, "Defending Christian Zionism – in response to Stephen Sizer and John Stott" TerraNova Publications 2008 (ISBN: 978-1-901949-62-9)

Alex Jacob, "The Case for Enlargement Theology" – Second Edition. ISBN: 9780-9551790-8-2, (Christian Publications International, 2012)

n.b. Alex Jacob is the CEO of CMJ (The Churches' Ministry Amongst Jewish People). Jacob has written several books which can be sourced through the CMJ website).

David Evans, "Christians and Israel – The Heart of the Matter" Tahilla Press, 2010 (ISBN: 978-1-907228-08-7)

Kelvin Crombie, "El Alamein – Halting a Possible Holocaust in the Middle East", ISBN: 978-0-9873630-1-5 (Mundaring, 2012)

Steve Maltz, "The Land of Many Names – Towards a Christian Understanding of the Middle East Conflict", ISBN: 1-86024-287-1 (Authentic, 2003)

(n.b. Steve Maltz's 30+ books cover many issues associated with the church, Israel, and the Hebraic root of the Christian faith. His publishing company is called "Saffron Planet Publishing").

Steve Maltz, "Hebraic Church" – Thinking Differently", ISBN: 9780-99319-10-46 (Saffron Planet Publishing, 2016)

Rob Richards, "Has God Finished With Israel? – a personal journey through biblical prophecy" ISBN:978-1-901949-67-4 (TerraNova, 2010)

Kelvin Crombie, "For the Love of Zion – Christian witness and the restoration of Israel" (ISBN:978-1-901949-63-6 (TerraNova, 2008)

Sandra Teplinsky, "Why Still Care About Israel? The Sanctity of Covenant, Moral Justice and Prophetic Blessing" ISBN:978-0-8007-9529-0, (Baker Publishing, 2013)

Joel Richardson, "When A Jew Rules The World – what the Bible really says about Israel in the plan of God" ISBN: 9781-938067-71-6, (WND Books, 2015).

David Pawson, "Israel in the New Testament", ISBN: 978-0-9823059-7-3 (True Potential Publishing, 2009)

Steve Maltz, "Shalom, God's Master Plan", ISBN: 9780-9931910-9-1, (Saffron Planet Publishing, 2019)

Lance Lambert, "The Eternal Purpose of God" ISBN: 9781-85240-5038 (Sovereign World Ltd, 2008)

David J Lambourn, "The Forgotten Bride – How the church betrayed its Jewish heritage" (available solely via Amazon)

Ken Burnett, "Why Pray for Israel?" ISBN: 978-18524-050-52 (Sovereign World, 2009)

Select list of books Peter Sammons

"The Empty Promise of Godism – Reflections on the multi-faith agenda" (2009)

"Rebel Church – a challenge and an encouragement to the Believer" (2013)

"The Messiah Pattern – the biblical feasts and how they reveal Jesus" (second edition, 2019)

(co-authored with David Serle) "Three Days and Three Nights – that changed the world" Sub-titled "Do the biblical accounts of the Resurrection agree?" (2018)

All available via Christian Publications International

Other useful books

David Pawson, "Unlocking the Bible" ISBN 978 0007 16666 4 (HarperCollins Publishers, 2015)

Simon Pease, "Ruth – A Prophetic Parable – how does the story of Ruth relate to you, today?" ISBN 9781-78926-512-5 (Christian Publications International, 2020)

David Lambourn, "Babel Versus Bible – The Battle for the Heart of Mankind", ISBN 978965241151 (available solely via Amazon).

Daniel Holland, "Prophetic Evangelism – Kingdom Exploits in the Risk Zone" (second edition) ISBN : 9781-91374-1-06-8 (Christian Publications International, 2021)

Rosemary Bamber, "In Time With God", ISBN: 97809572871-1-2
(In Time With God Publications, 2012) (a 366-day bible study with daily readings according to the days / times of year that biblical events actually occurred)

Alfred Edersheim, "The Life and Times of Jesus the Messiah" ISBN: 0-943575-83-4 (Hendrickson Publishers, 1997) (An up-dated and simplified version: "*Jesus: Life & Times - A Clash of Kingdoms*" ... and "*The Triumph of Mercy*", 2022, edited by Steve Maltz, ISBN 978-1-9163437-4-0. Due out 2022 via Saffron Planet Publishing)

Baker Encyclopedia of the Bible, ISBN 0-8010-2139-1. Four volume set.
(Baker Book House Company, 1997).

One New Man Bible, ISBN 978-1-935769-11-8 (True Potential Publishing, Inc, 2011)

Philip Wren, "Revelations of Jesus Christ - From the book of Revelation - a devotional study", ISBN 9781-78926-5118, Christian Publications International, 2019.

Paul Langham, "Understanding Revelation - A preacher looks at the end-time message of the last book of the Bible", ISBN 1901-94935-4, Terra Nova Publications, 2005.